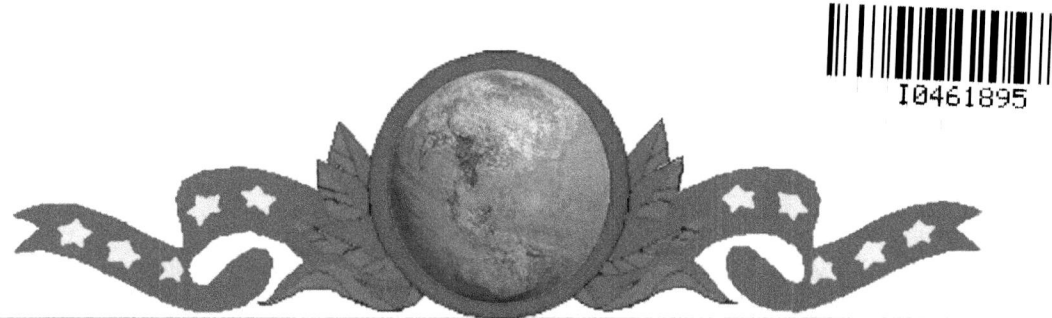

Real World
Colouring Book
For Advanced Users & Adults

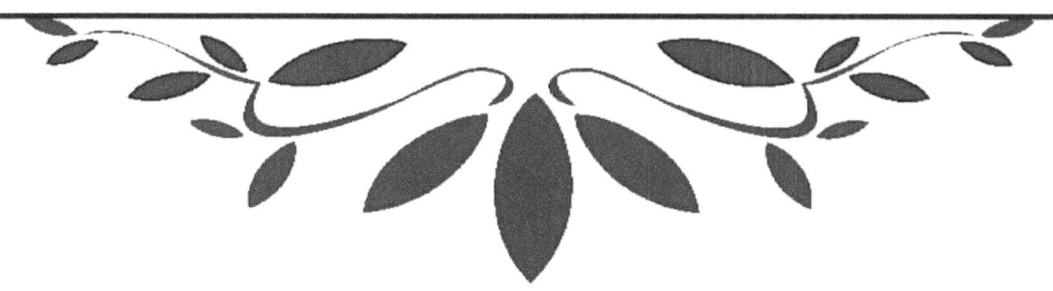

Copyright 2019 By John Boom

50 Images

Created From Real Life Photos
For You To Colour As You Please.

ISBN 978-0-359-97234-0

9 780359 972340

90000

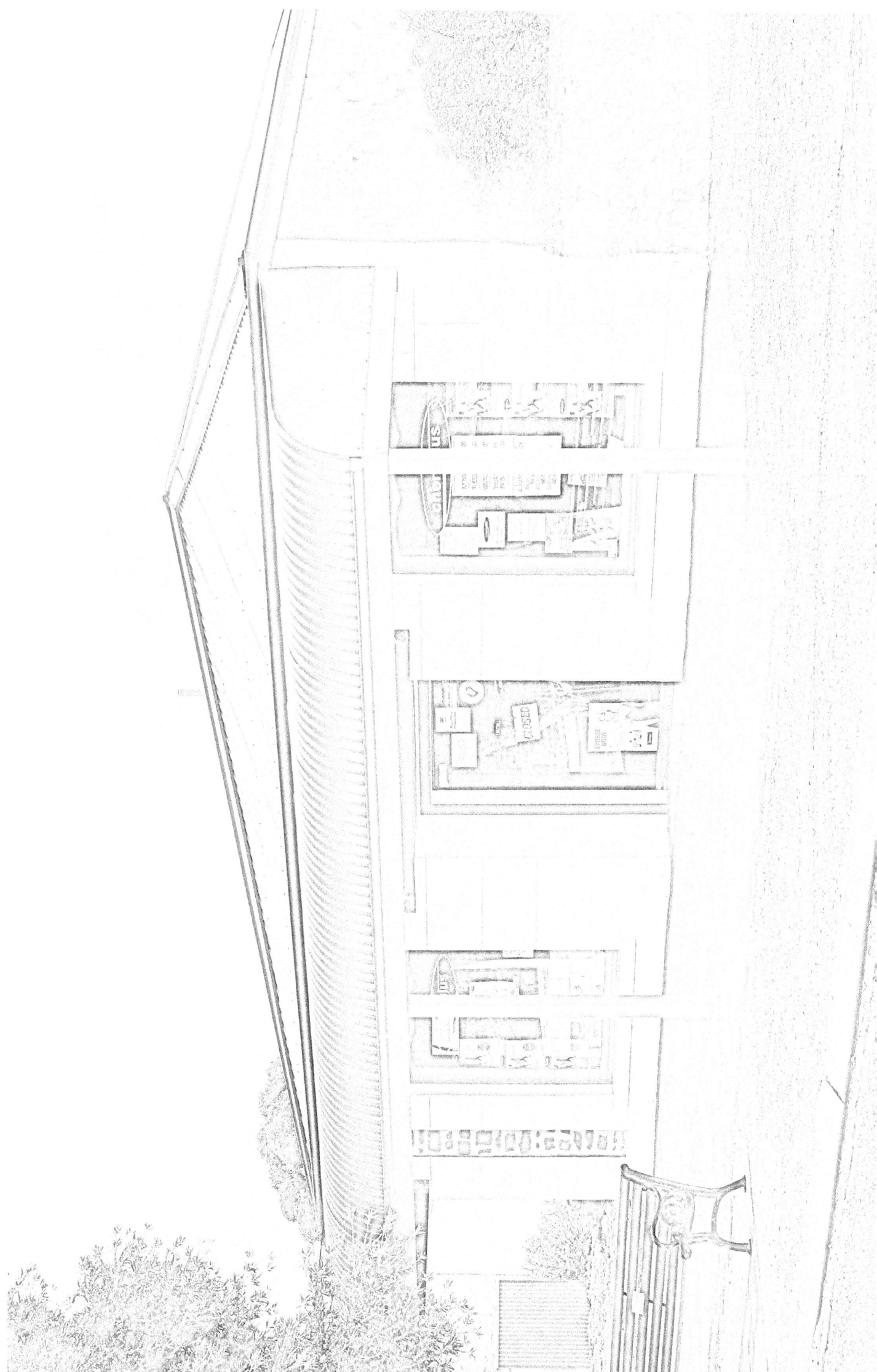

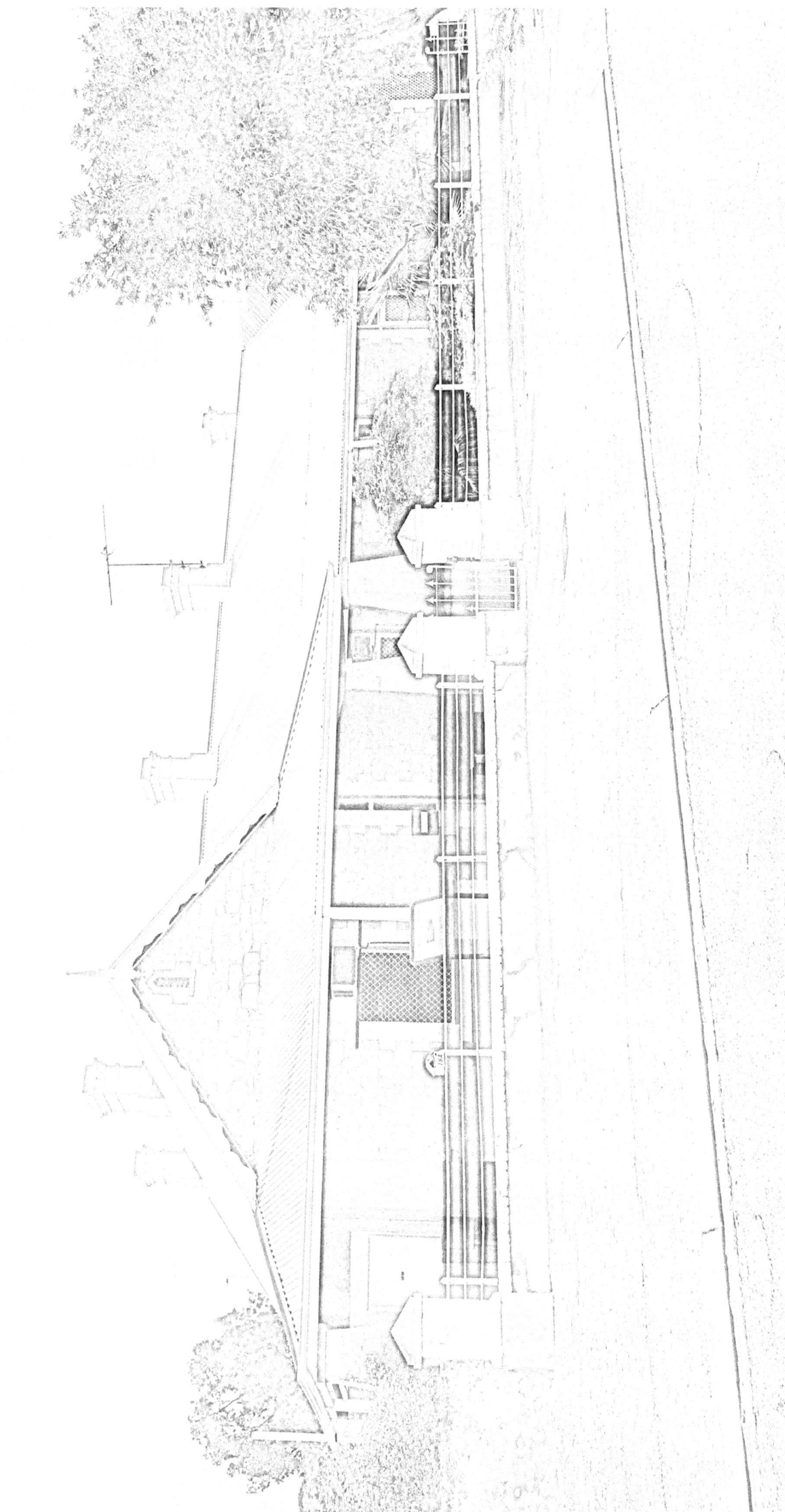

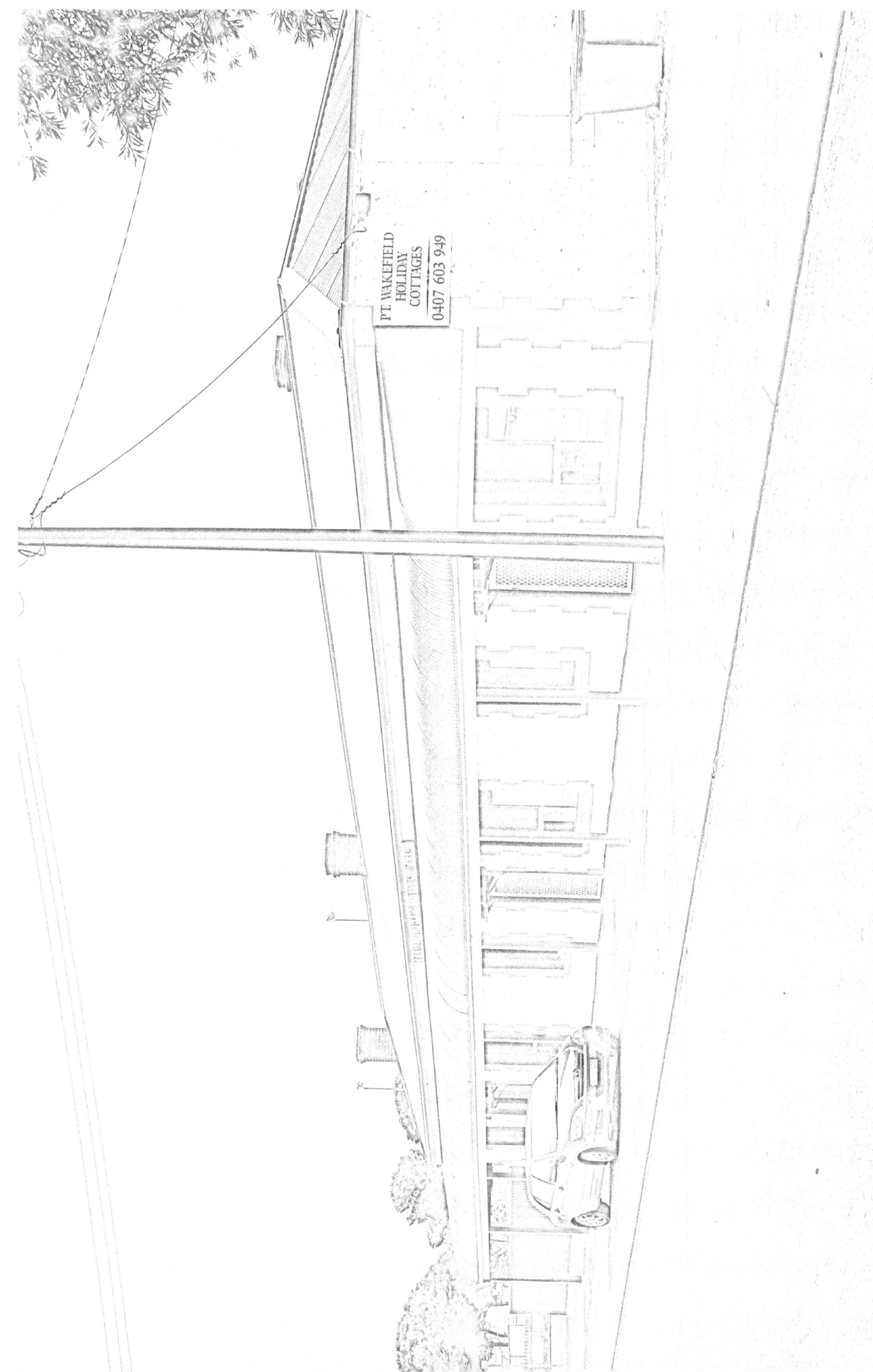

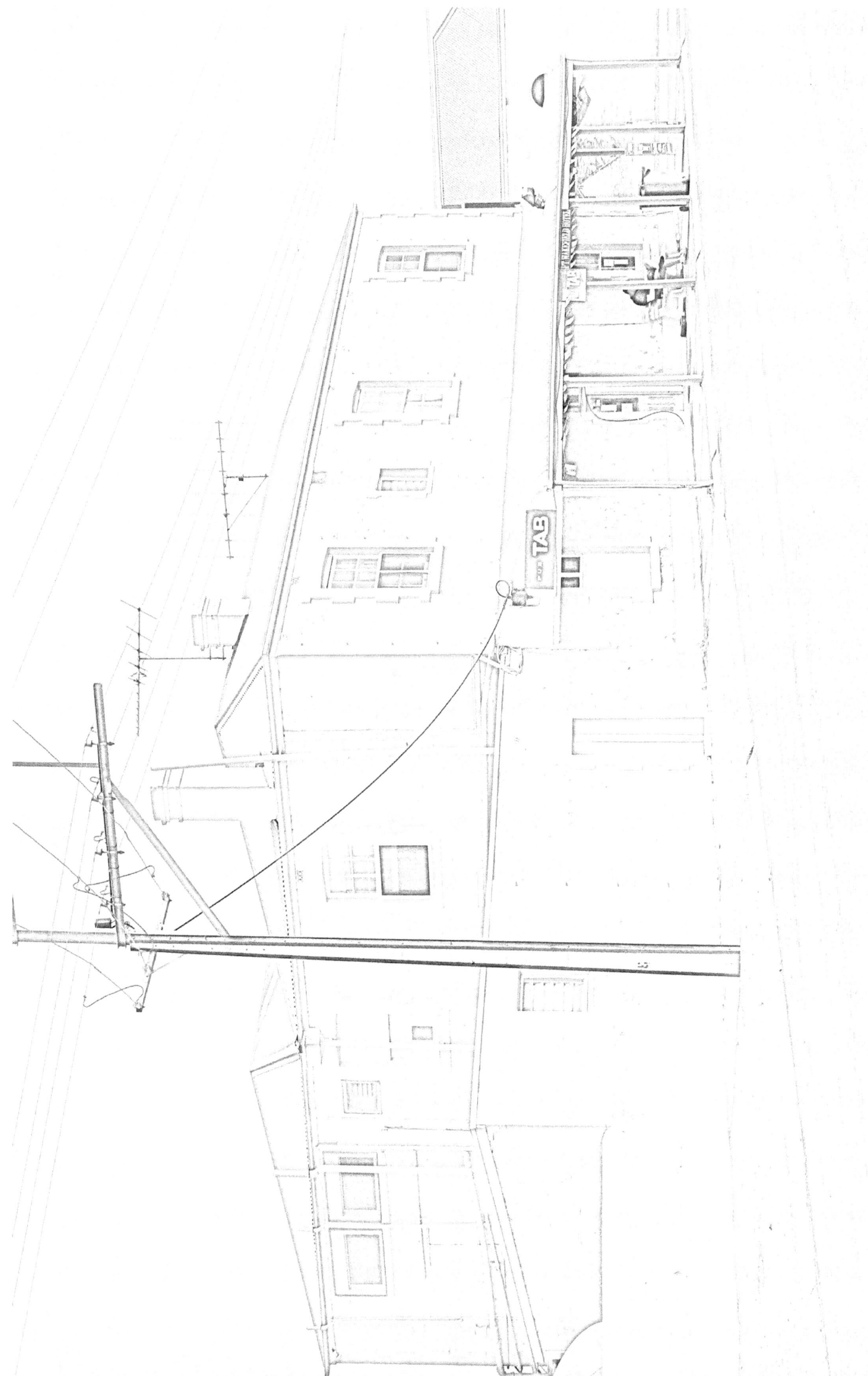

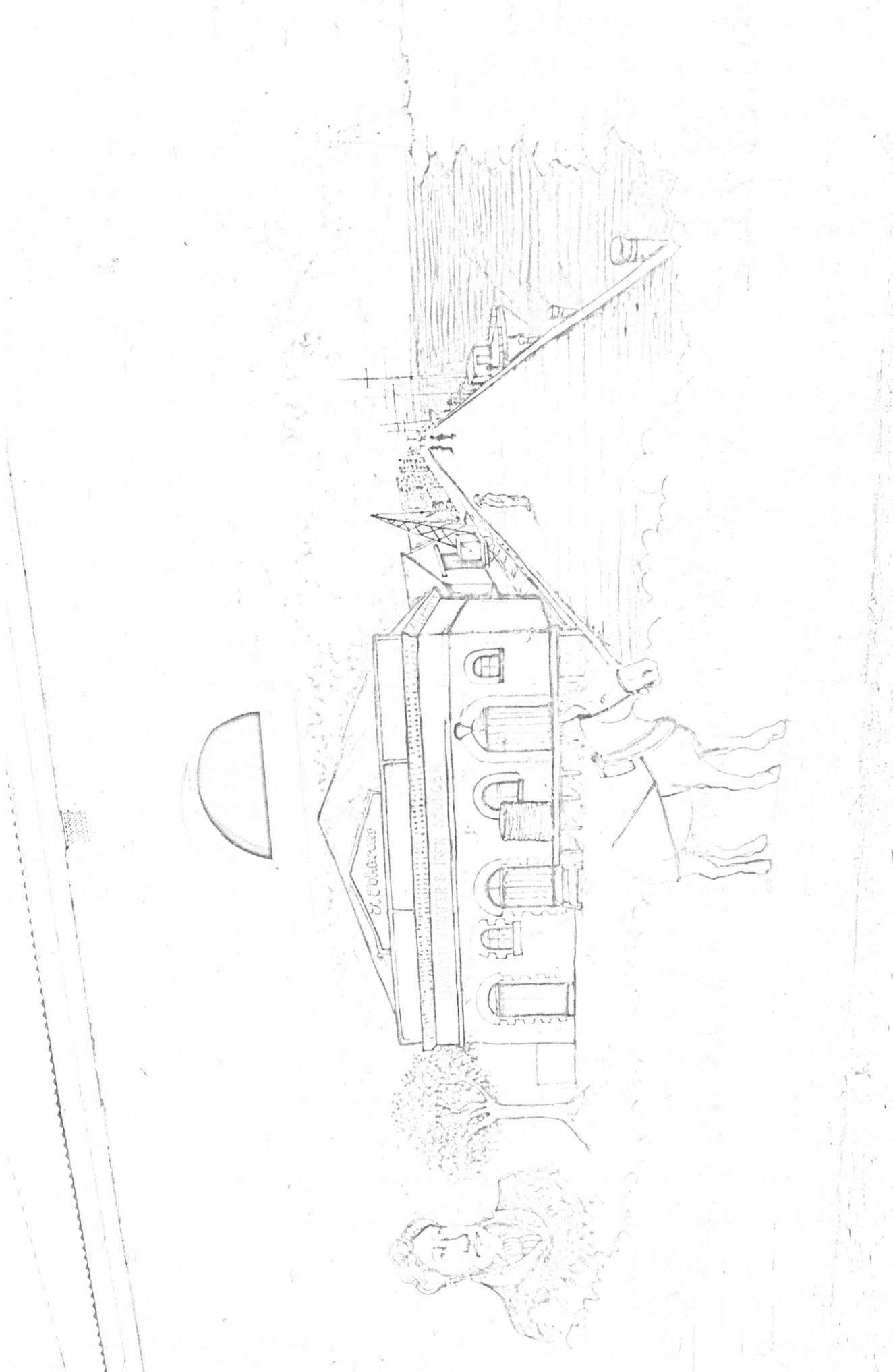

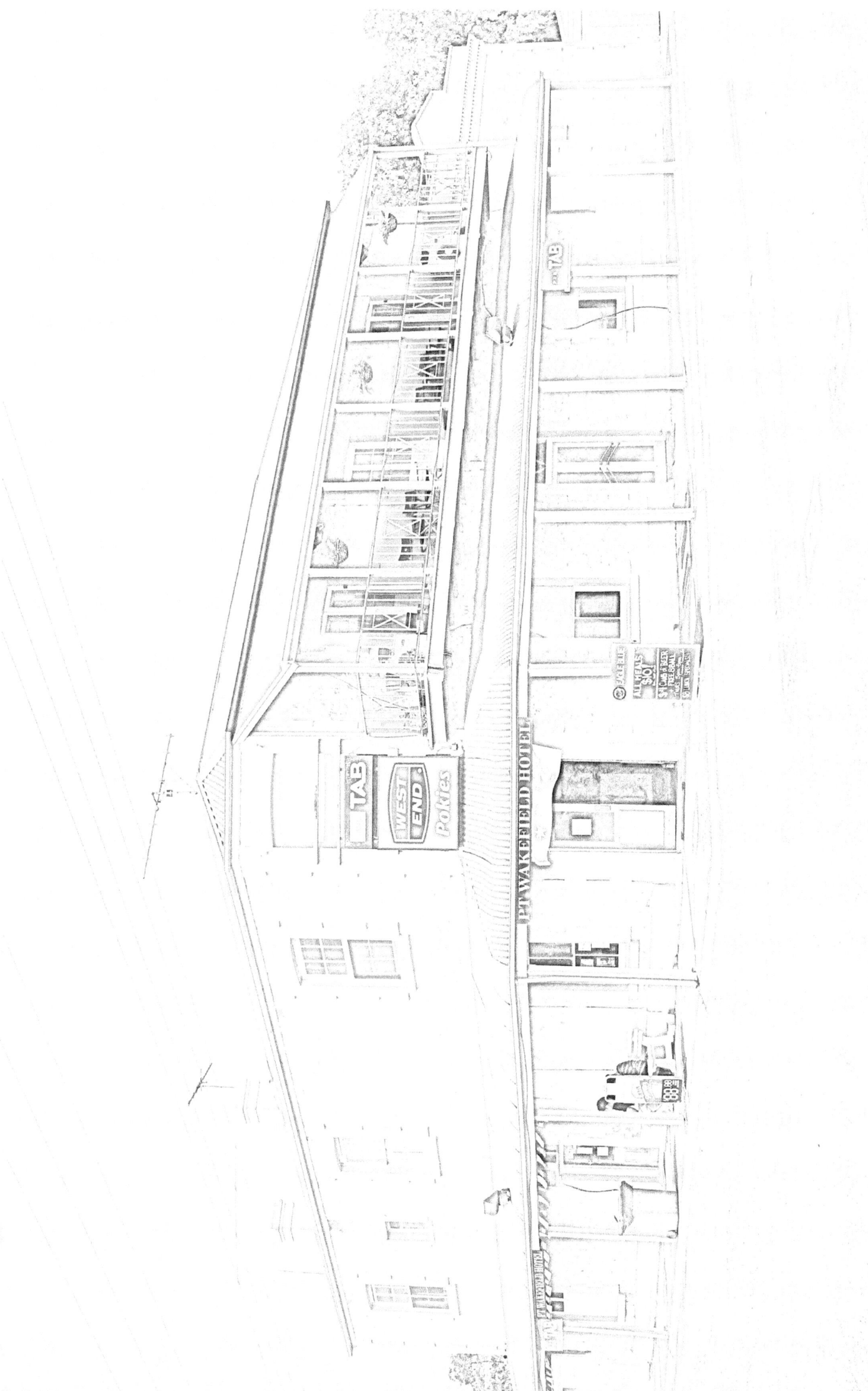

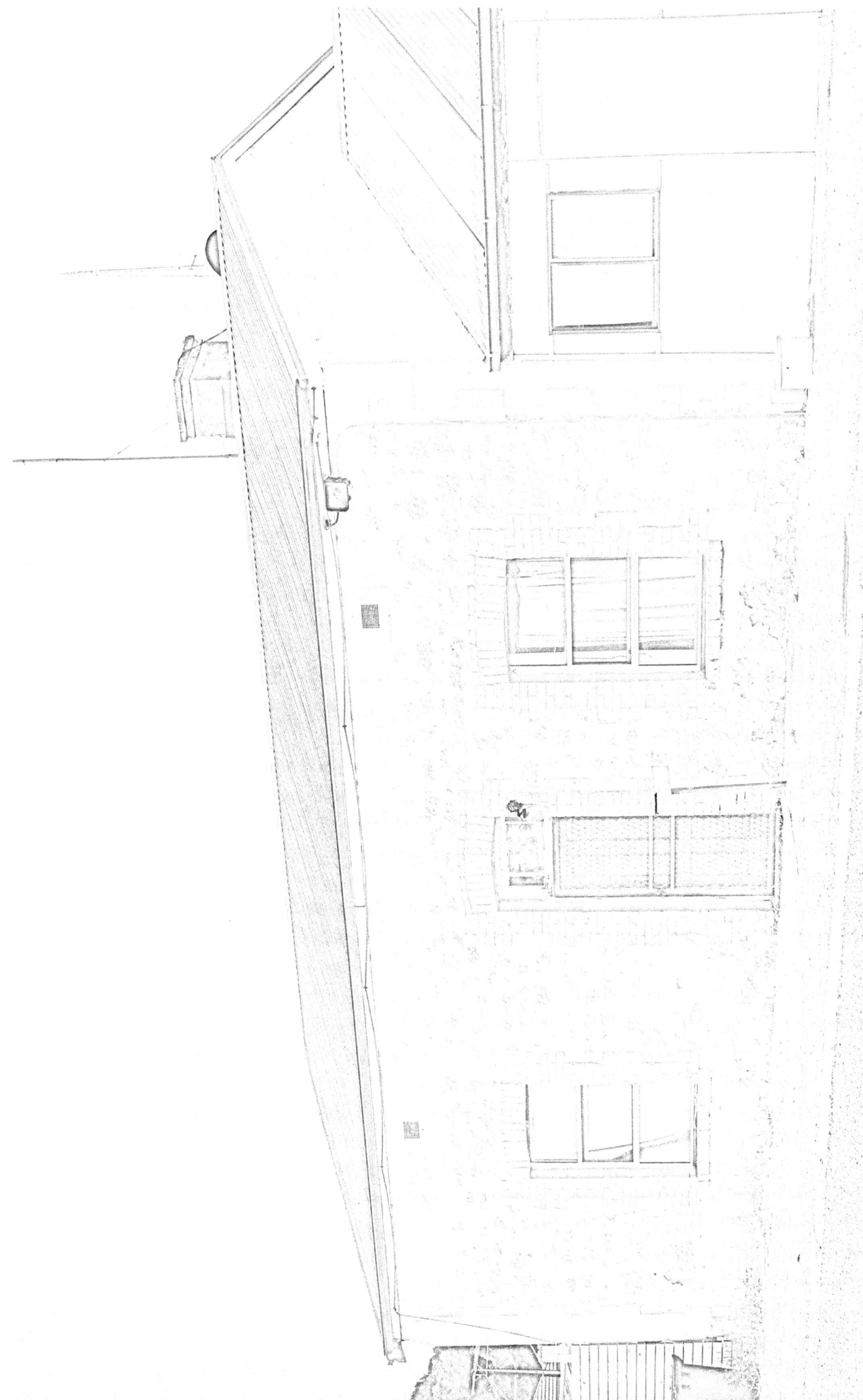

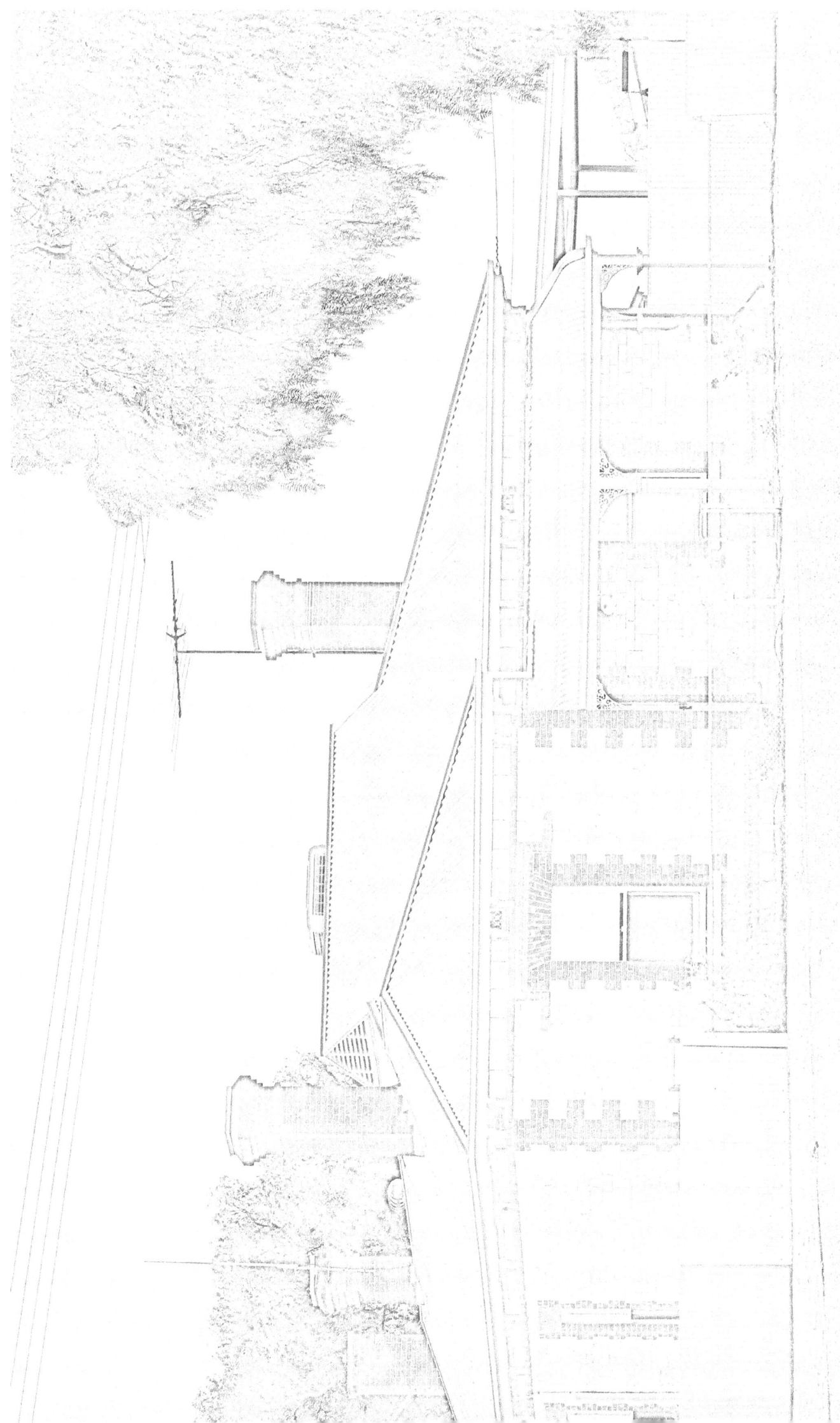

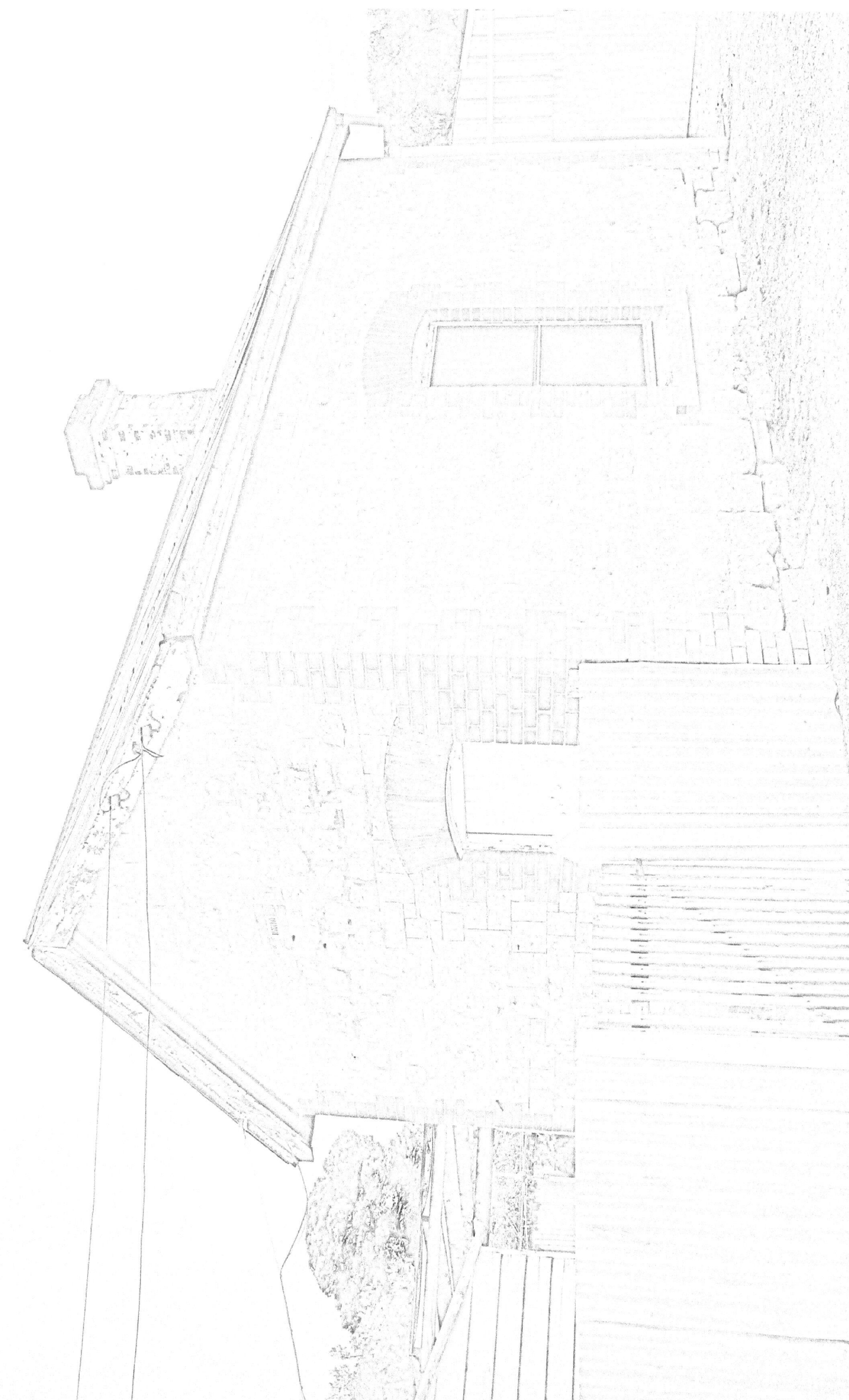

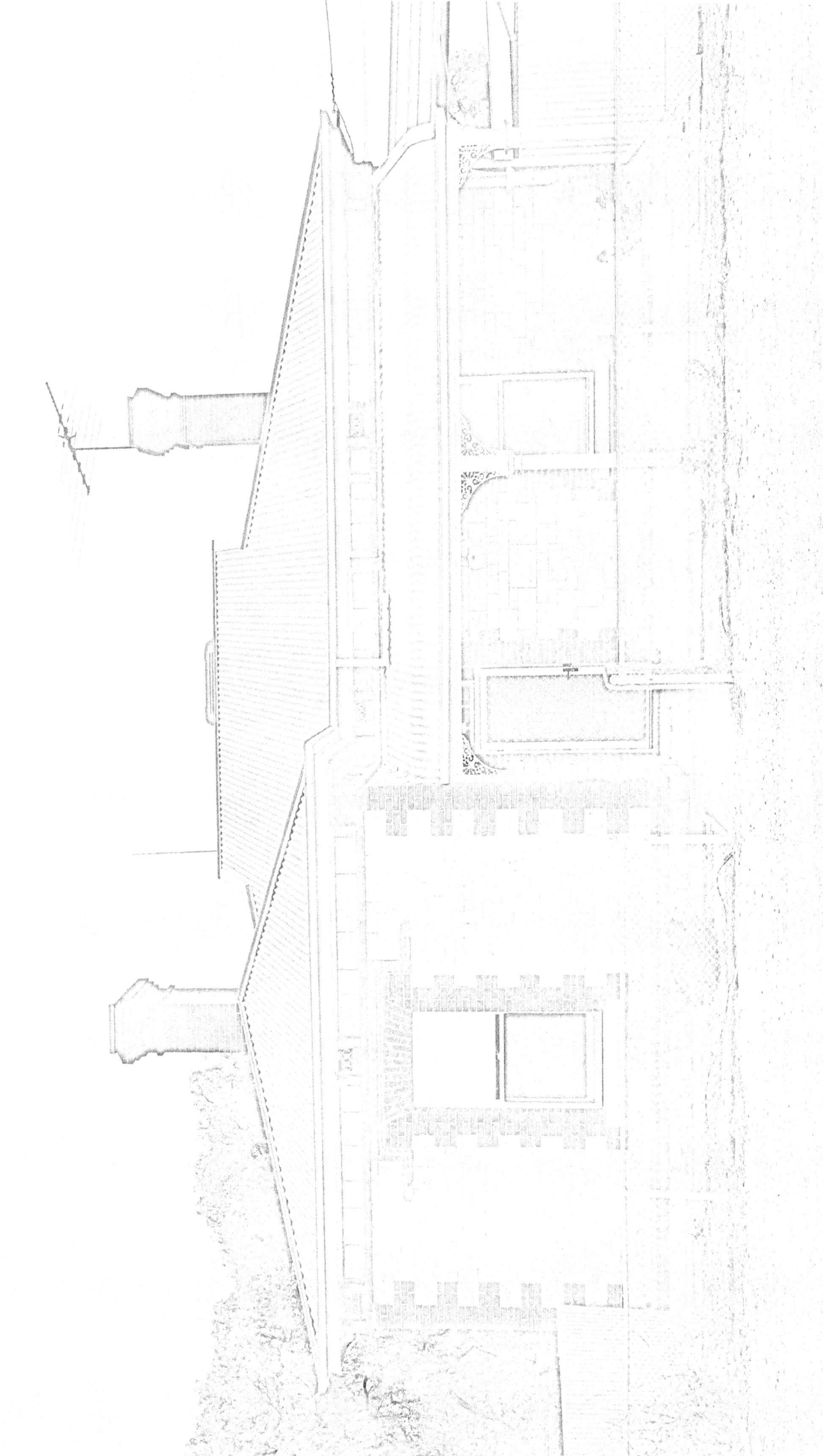

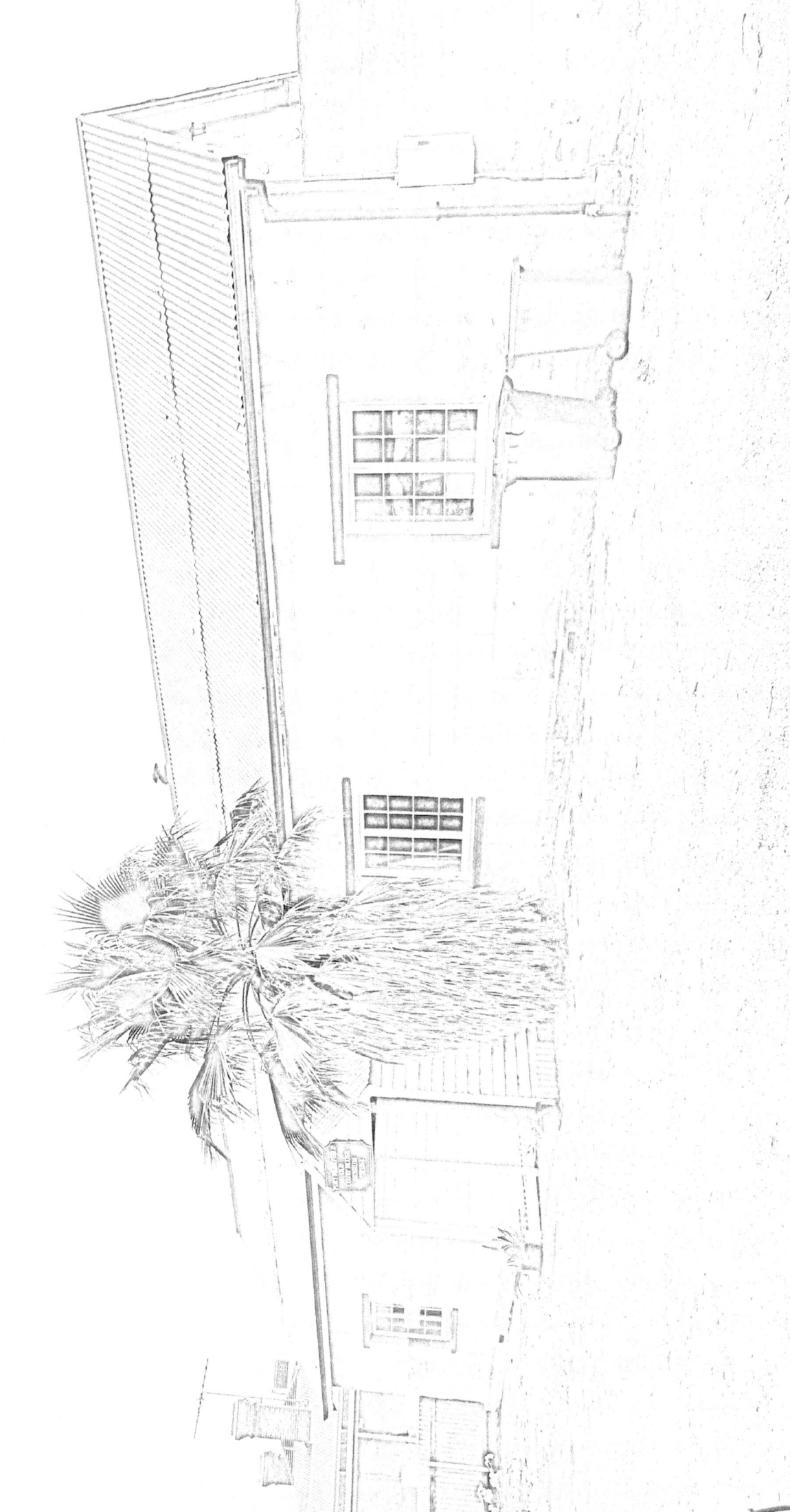

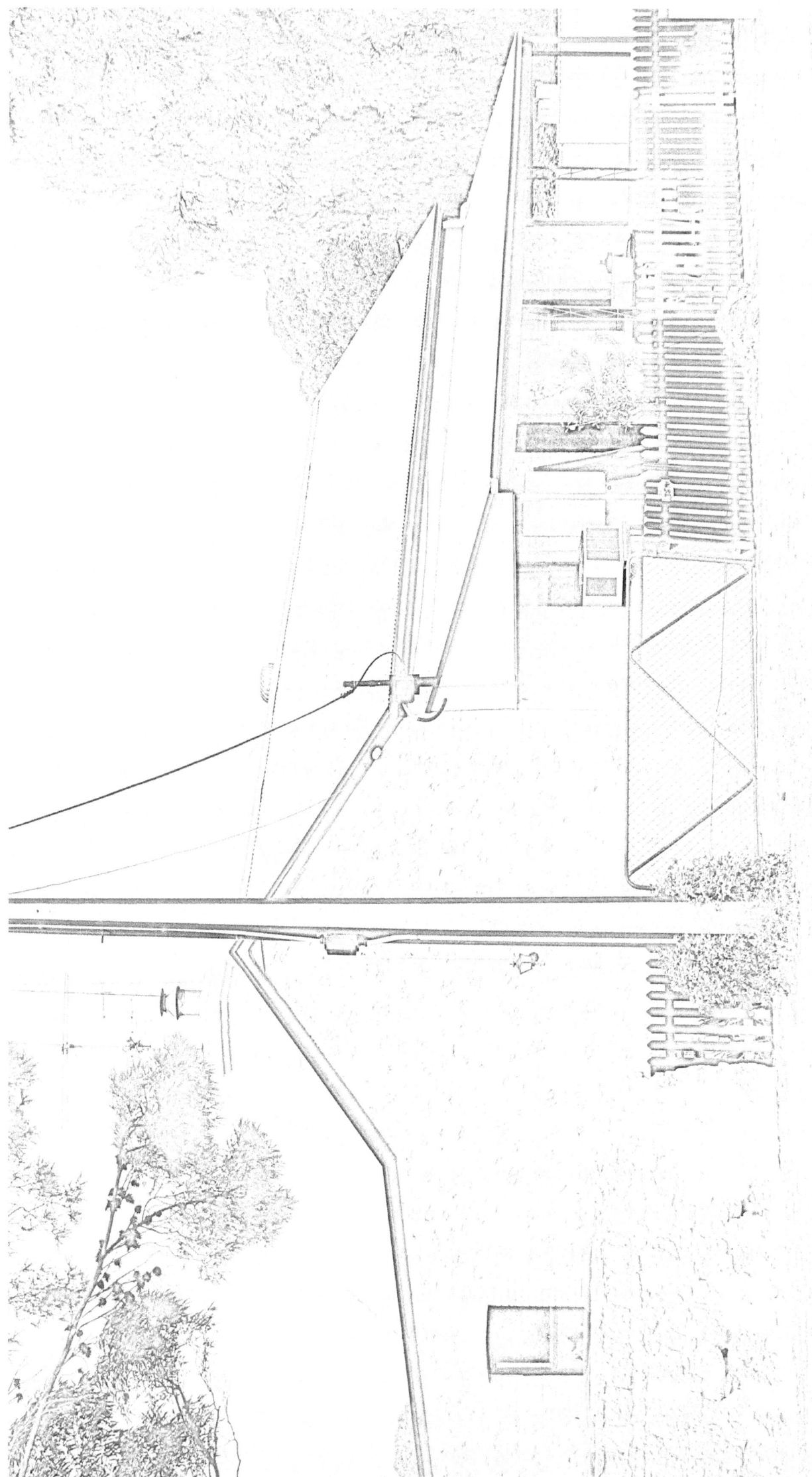

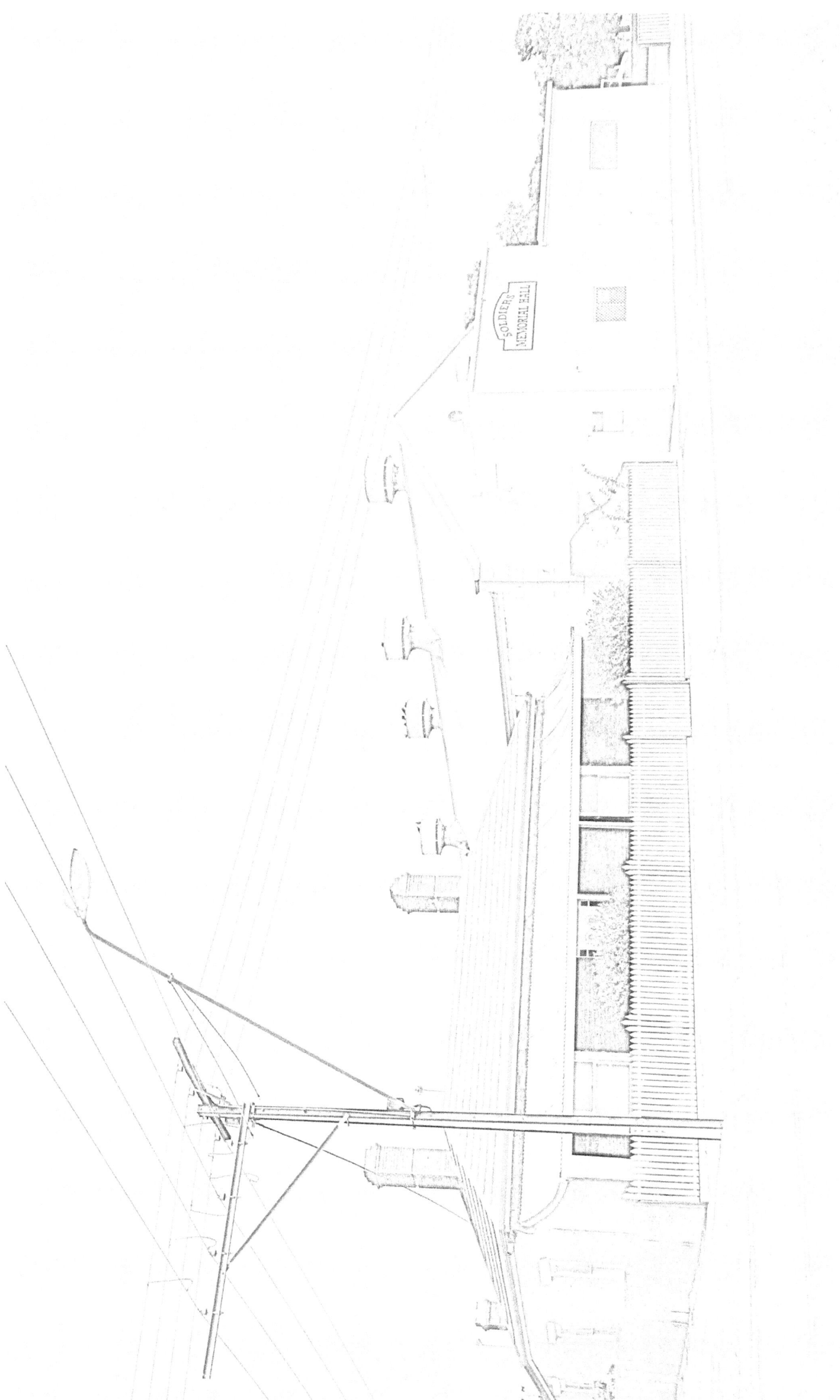

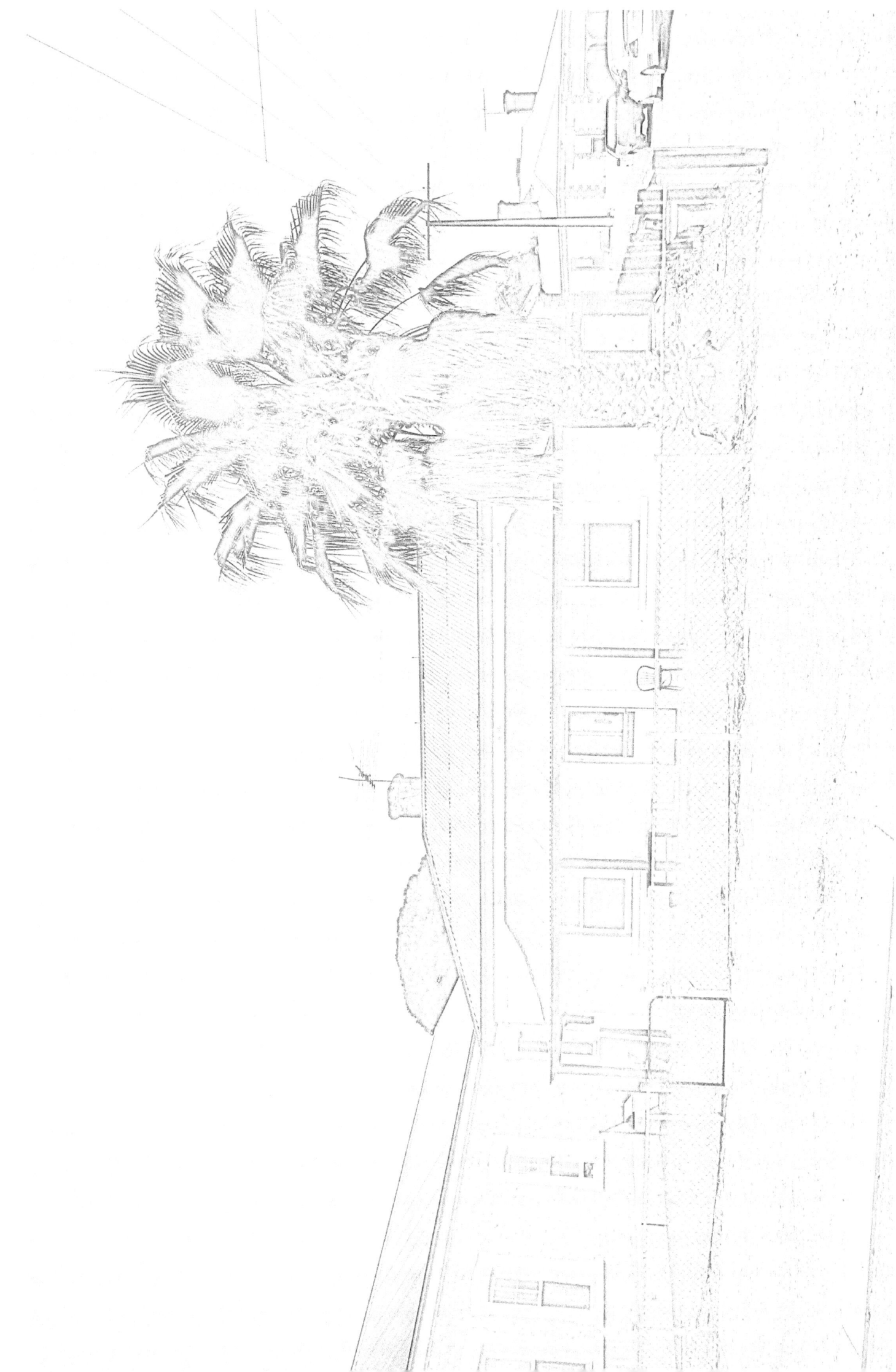

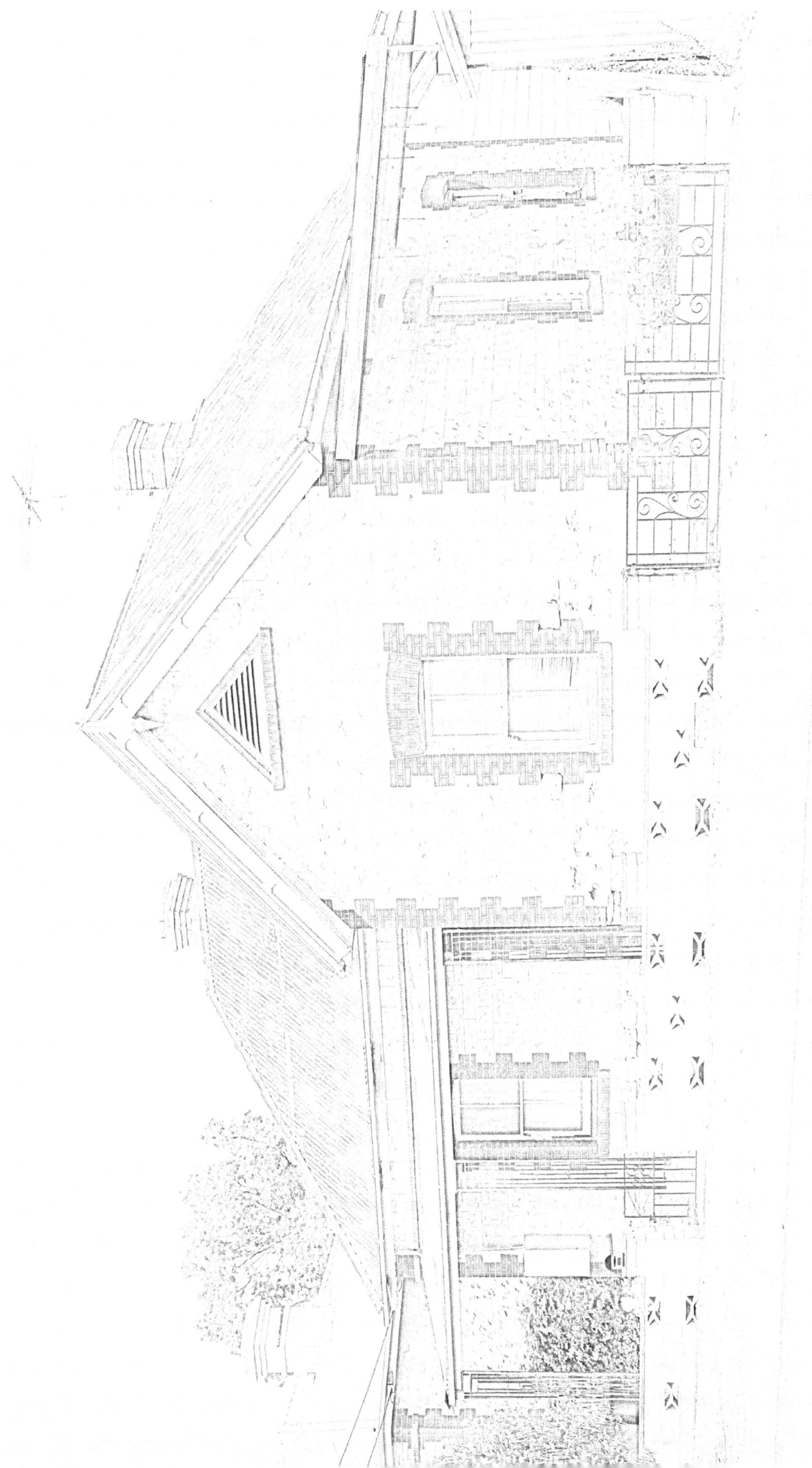

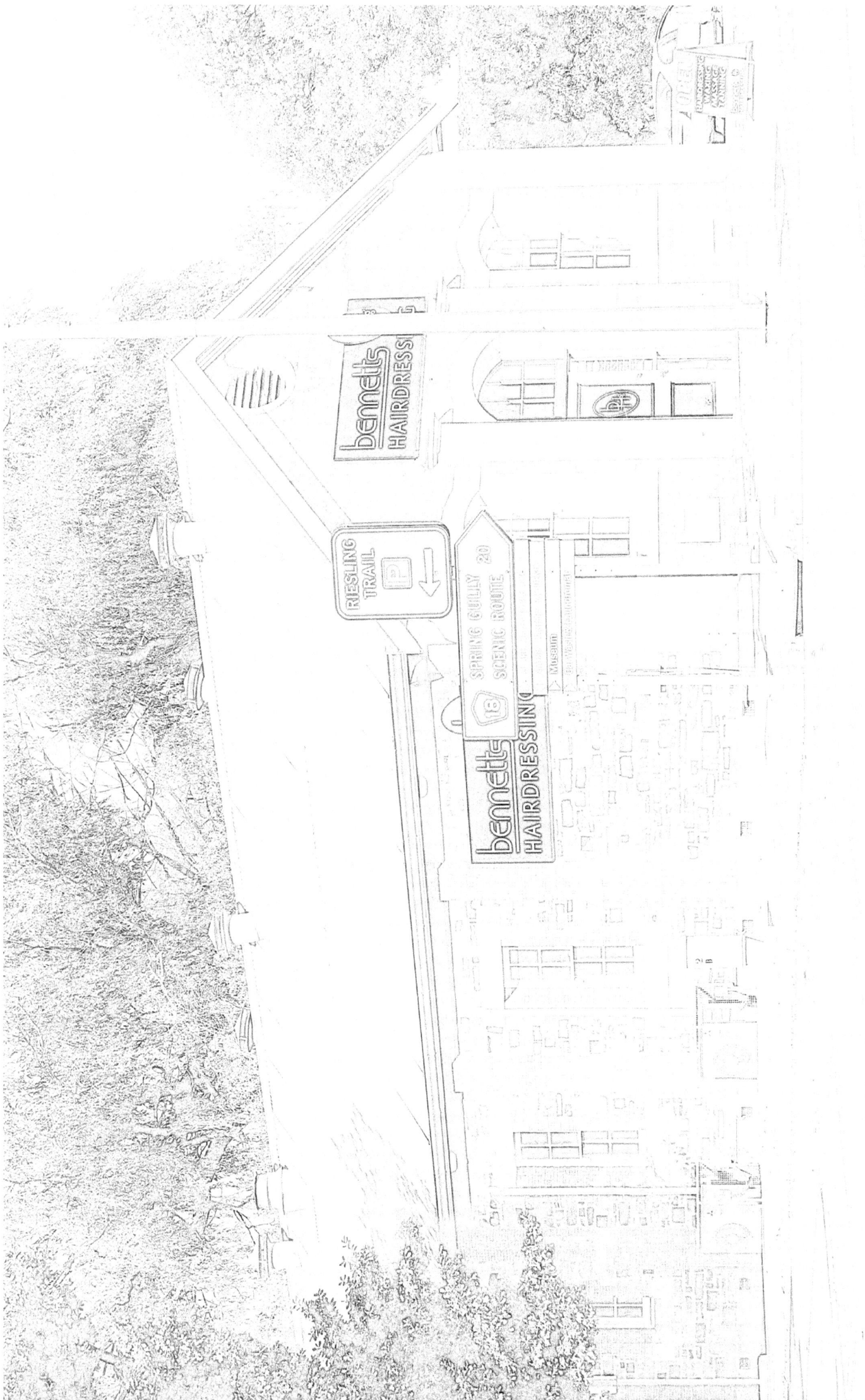

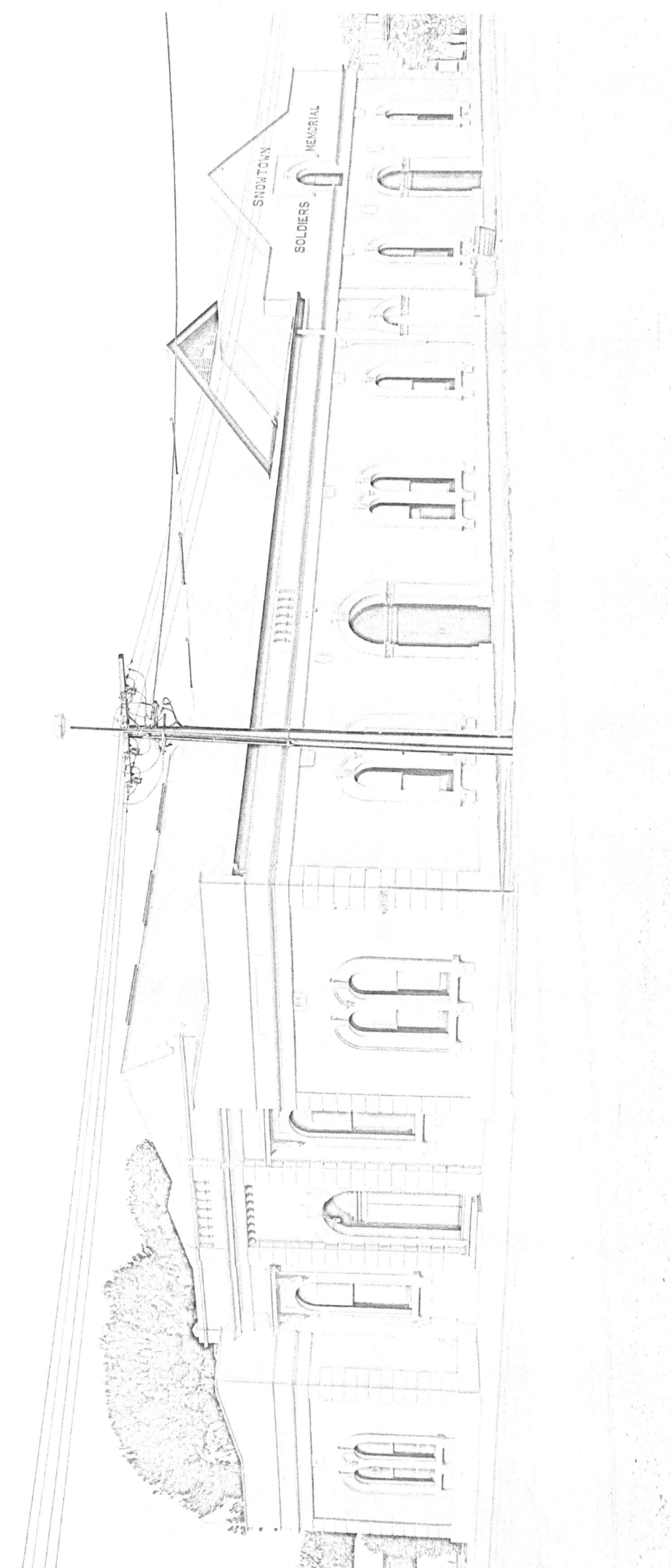

SNOWTOWN SOLDIERS MEMORIAL

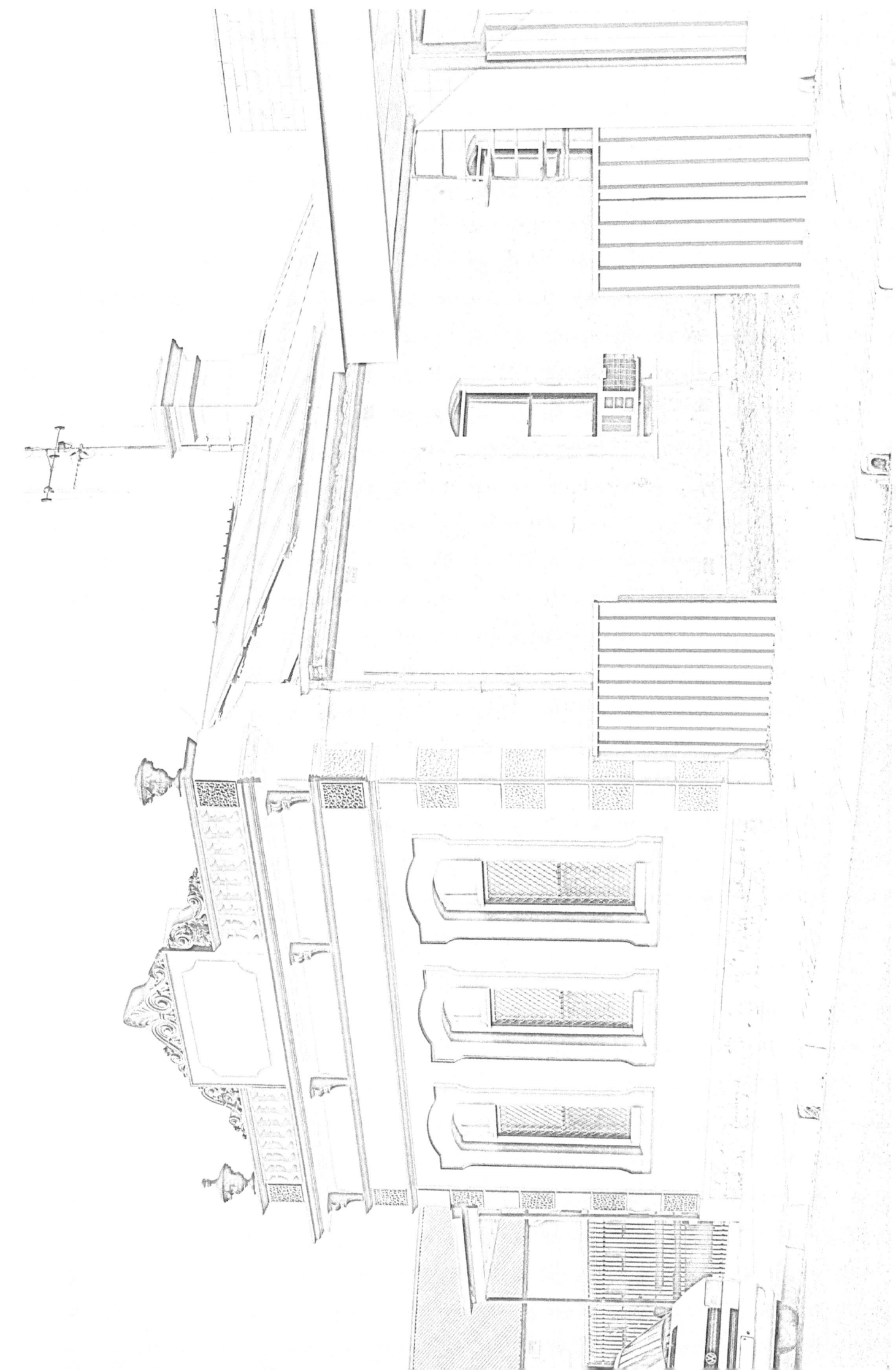

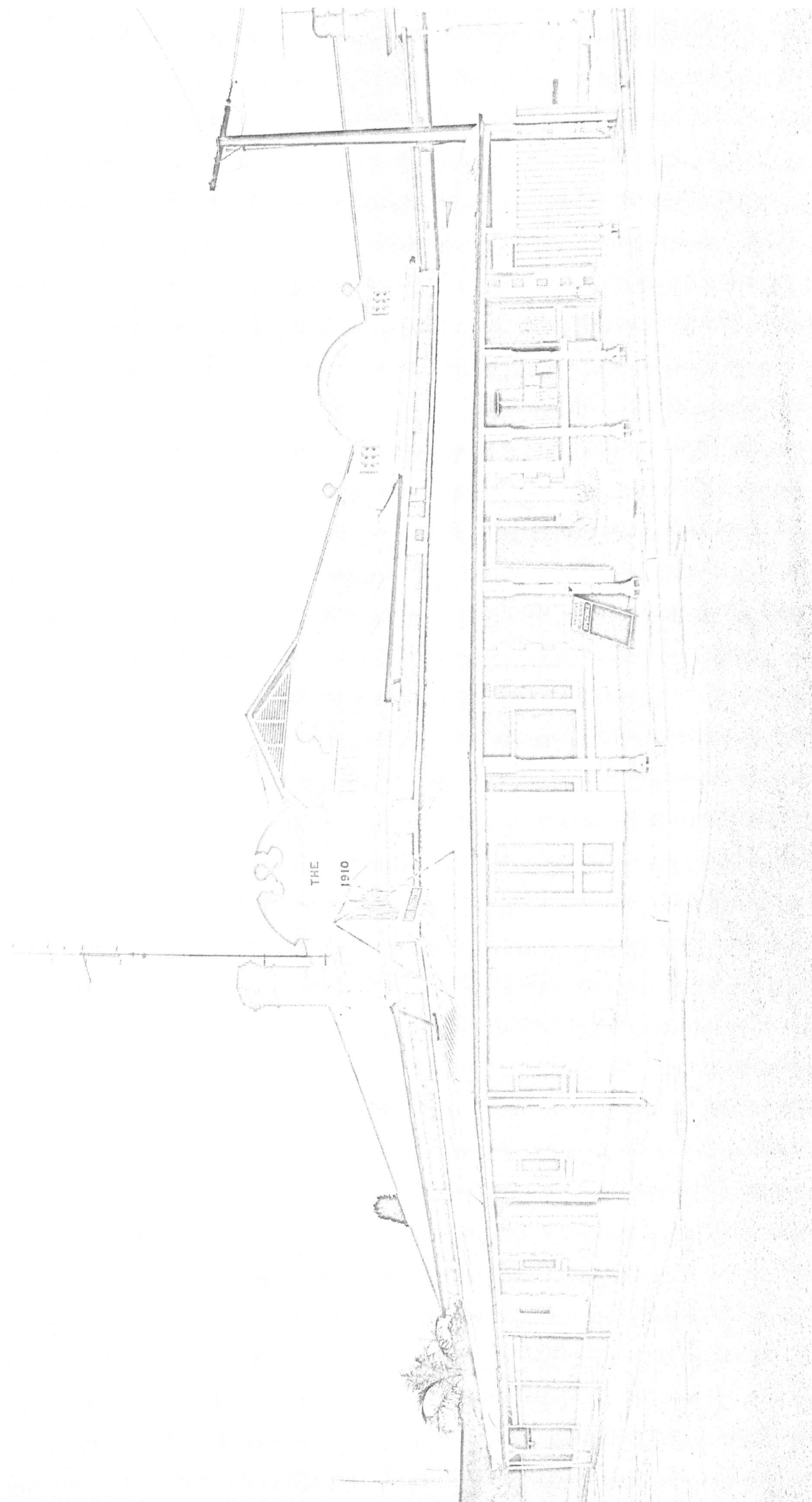

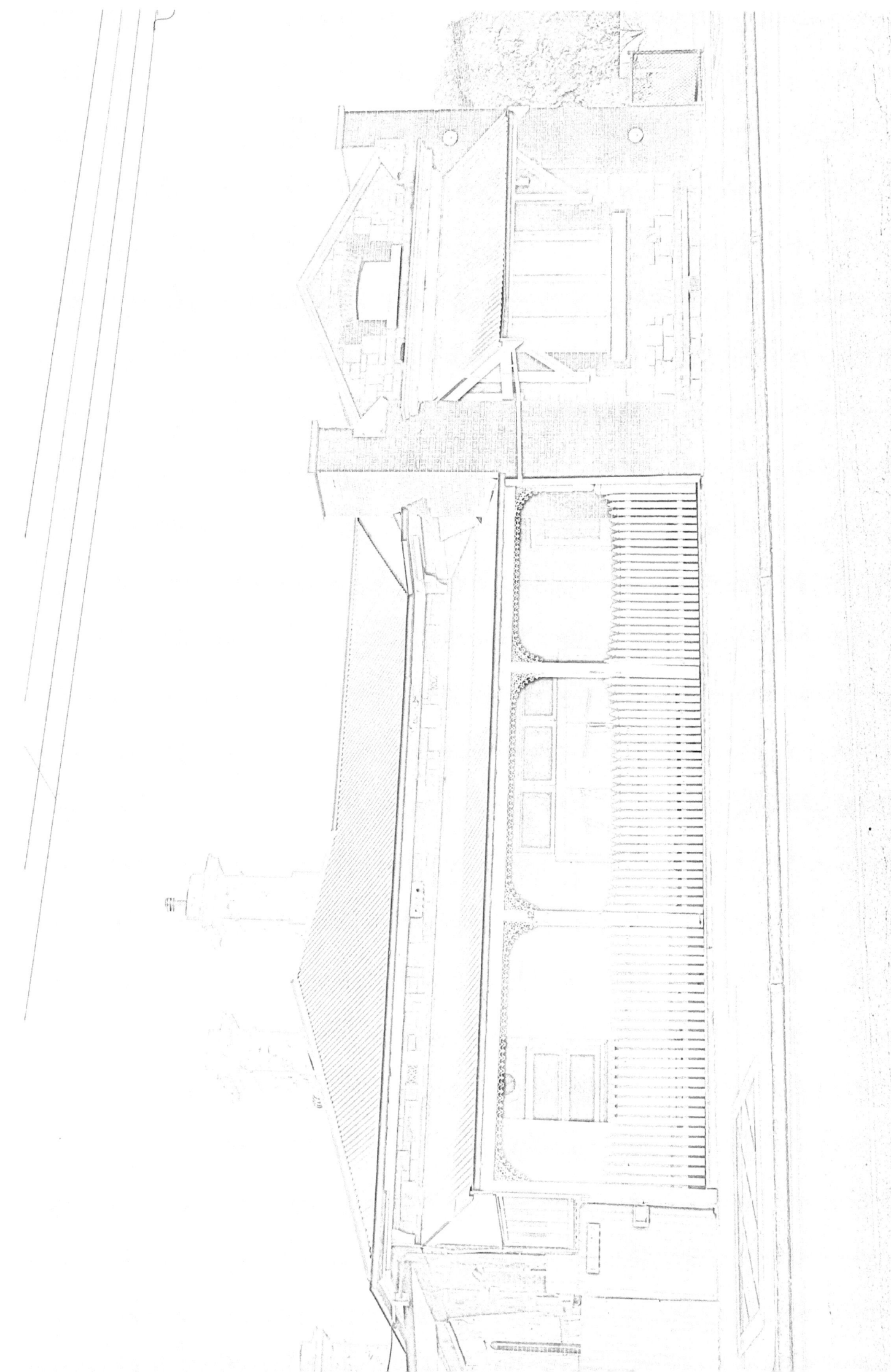

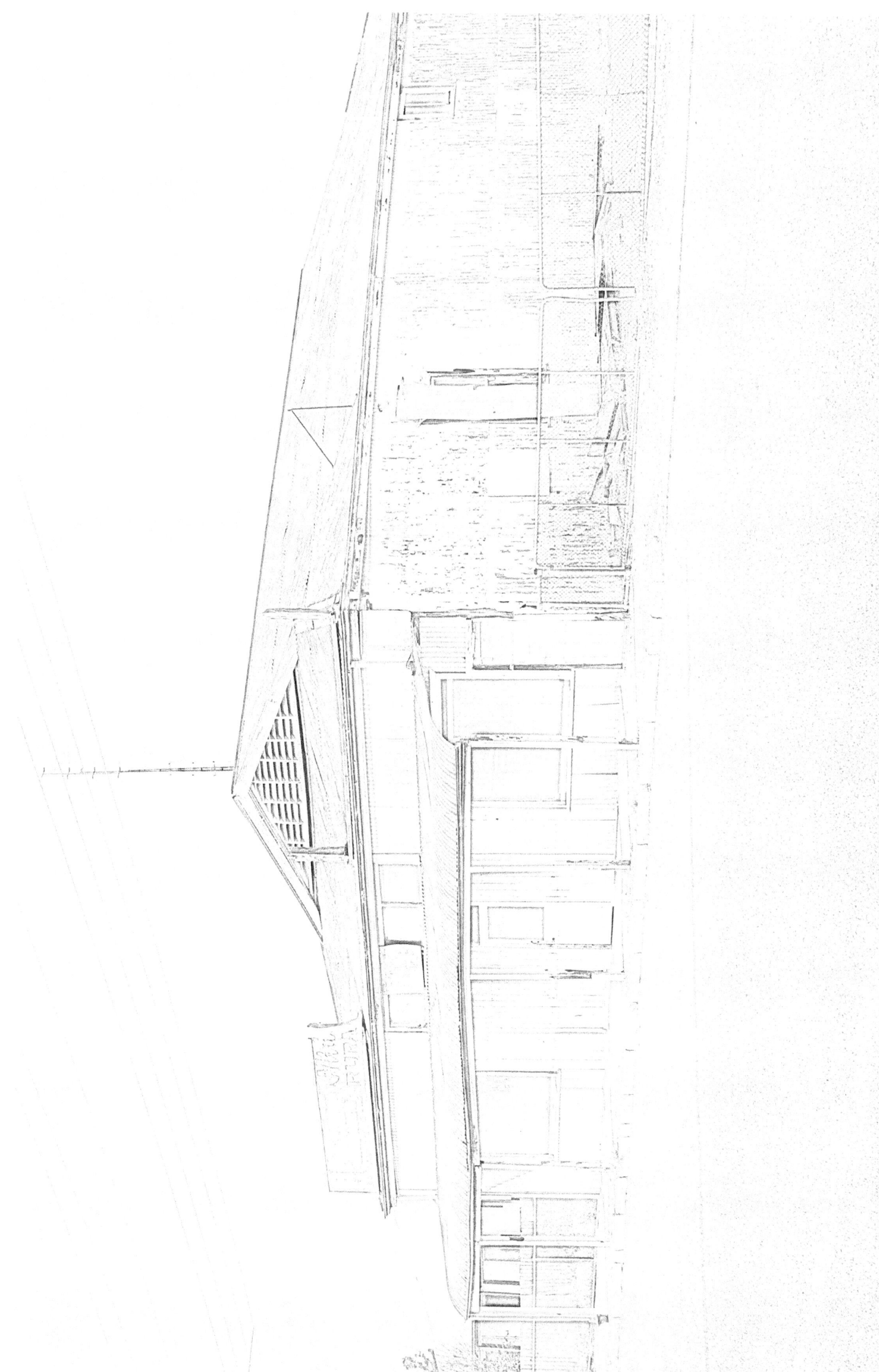

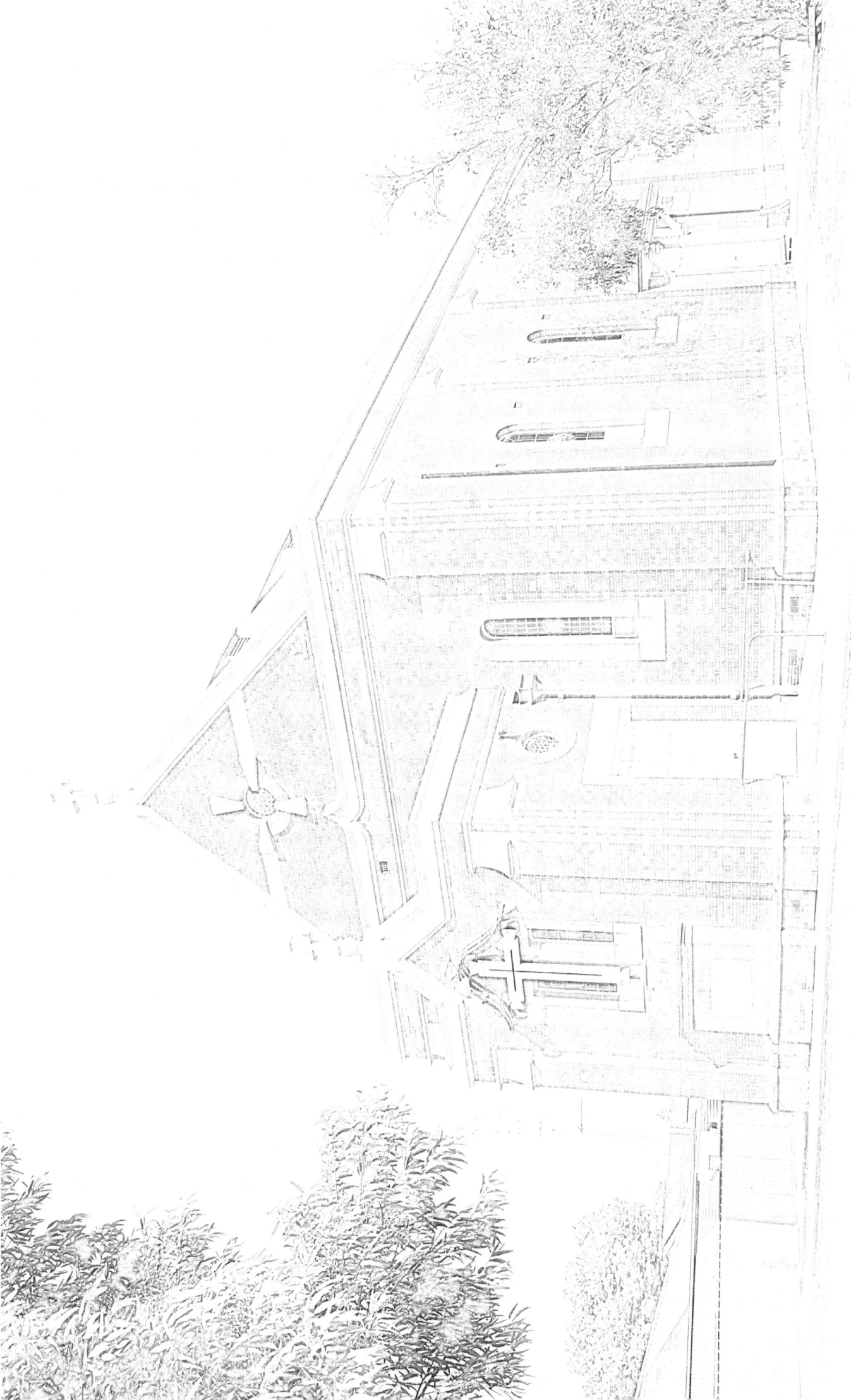

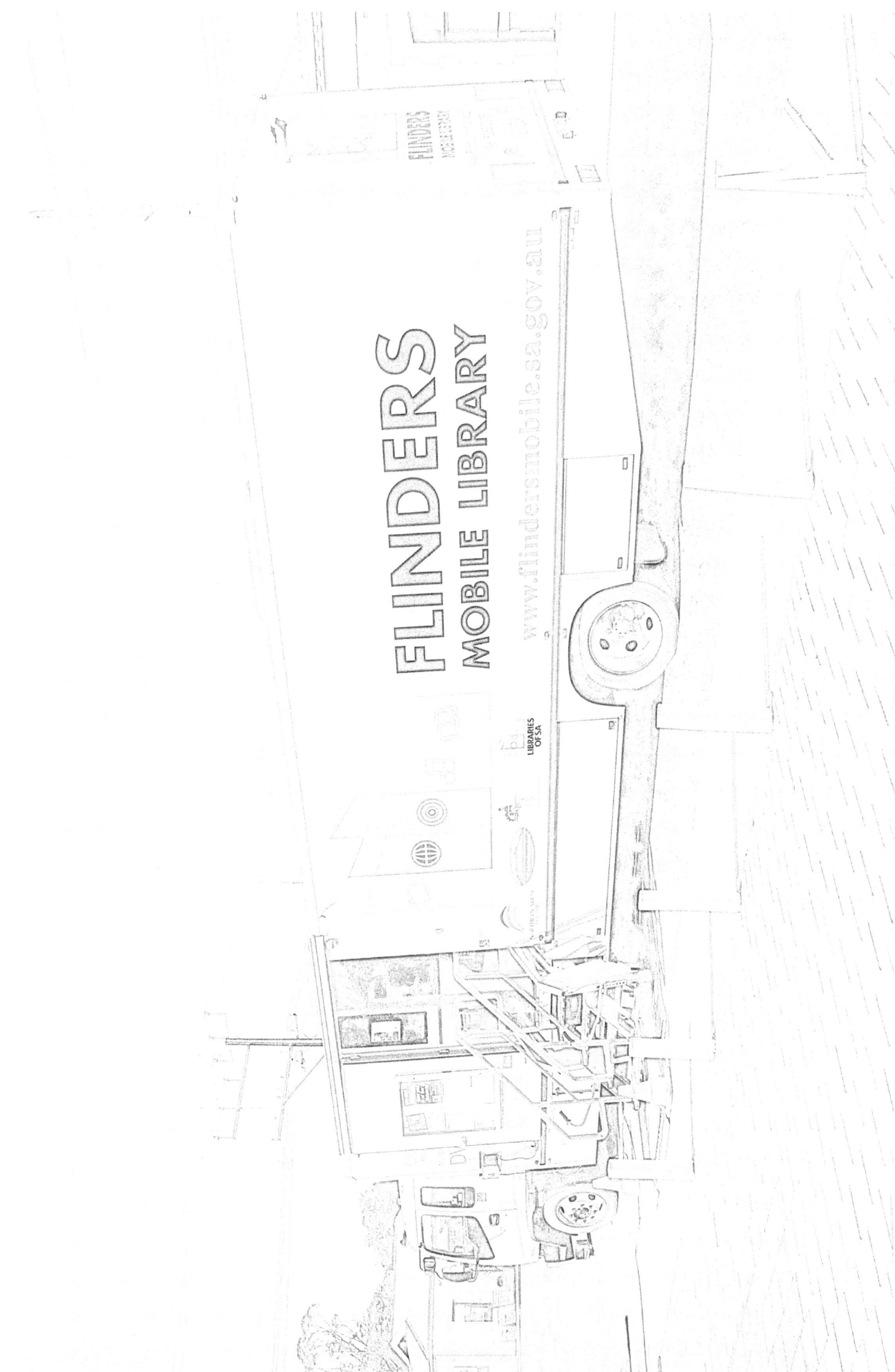

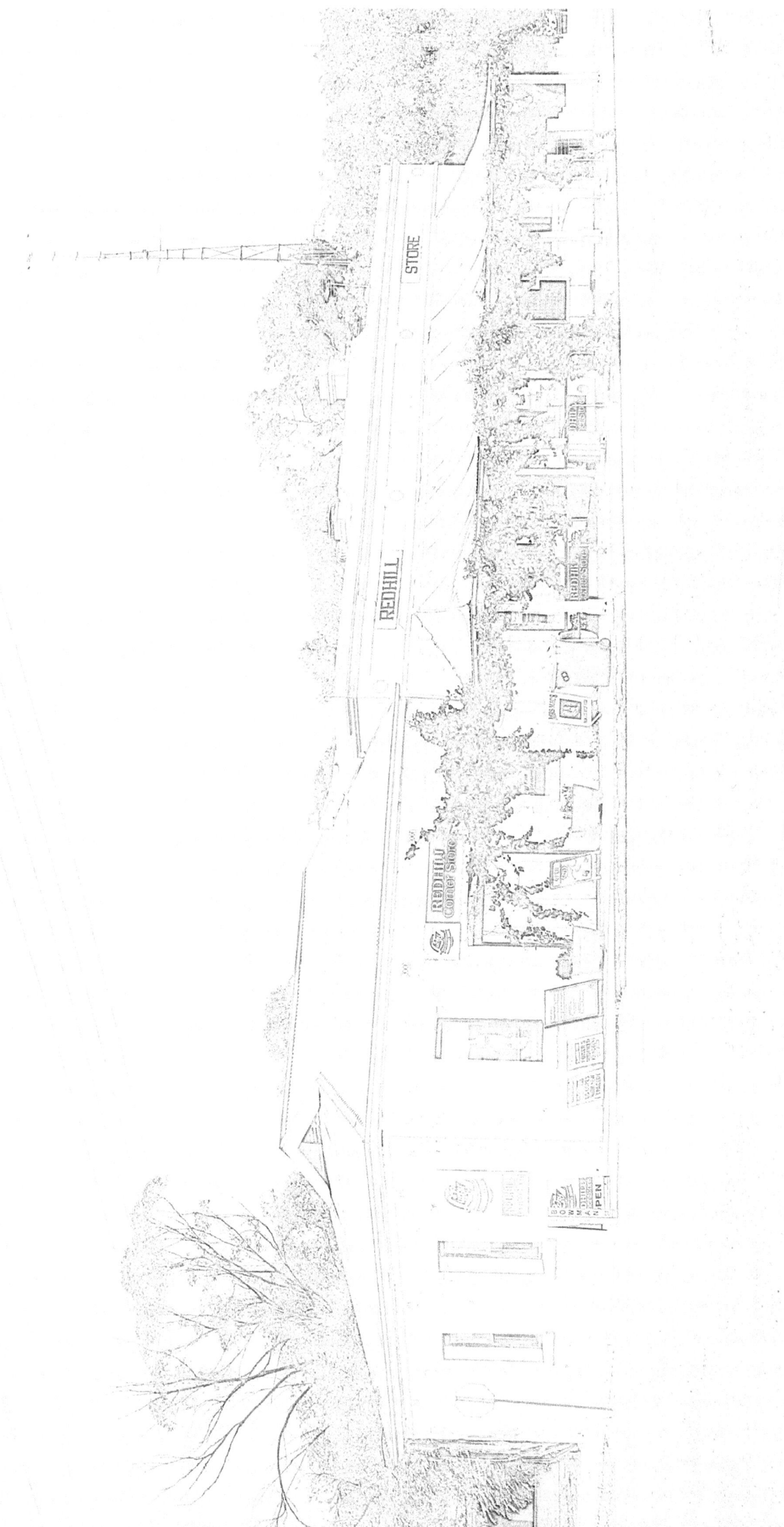

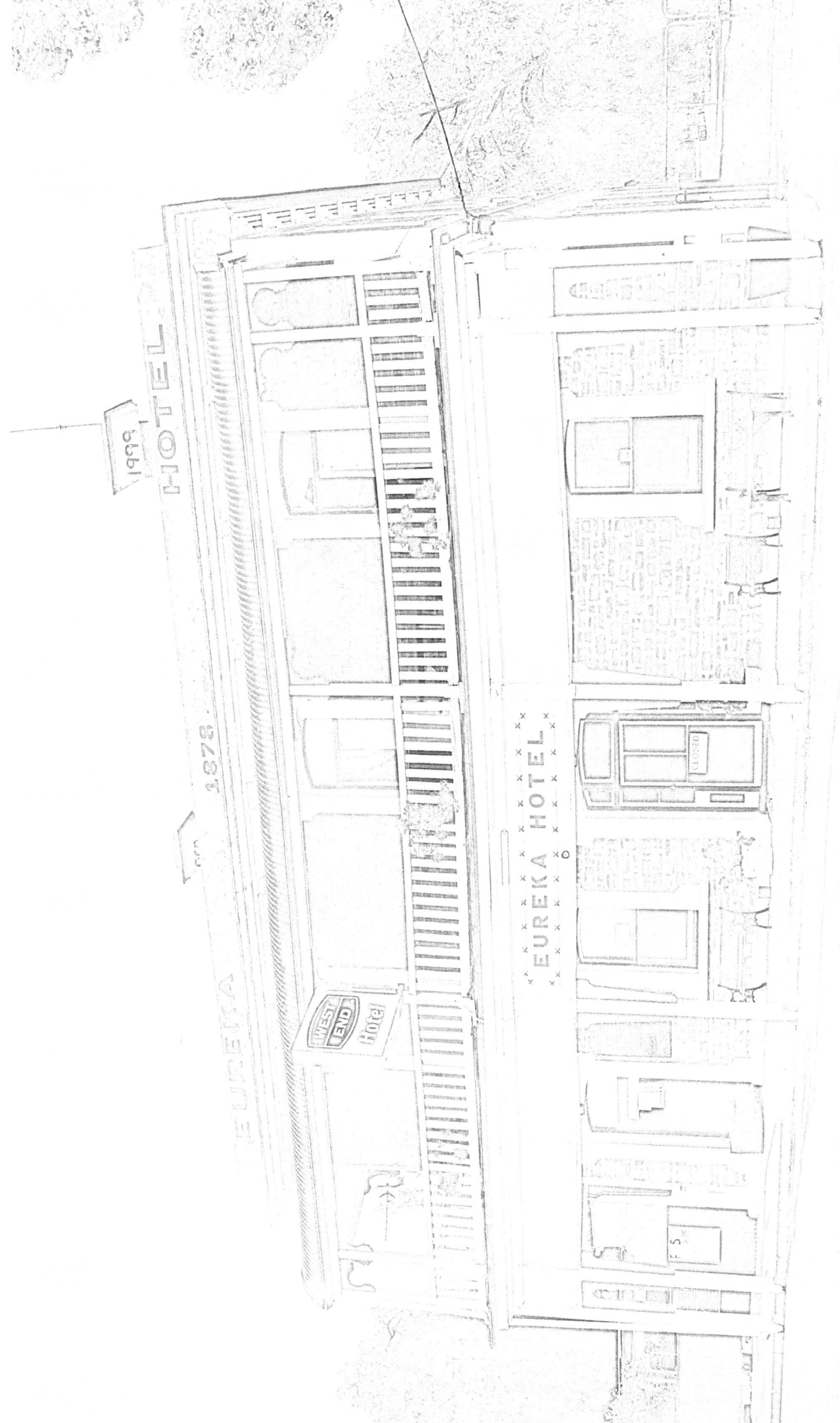

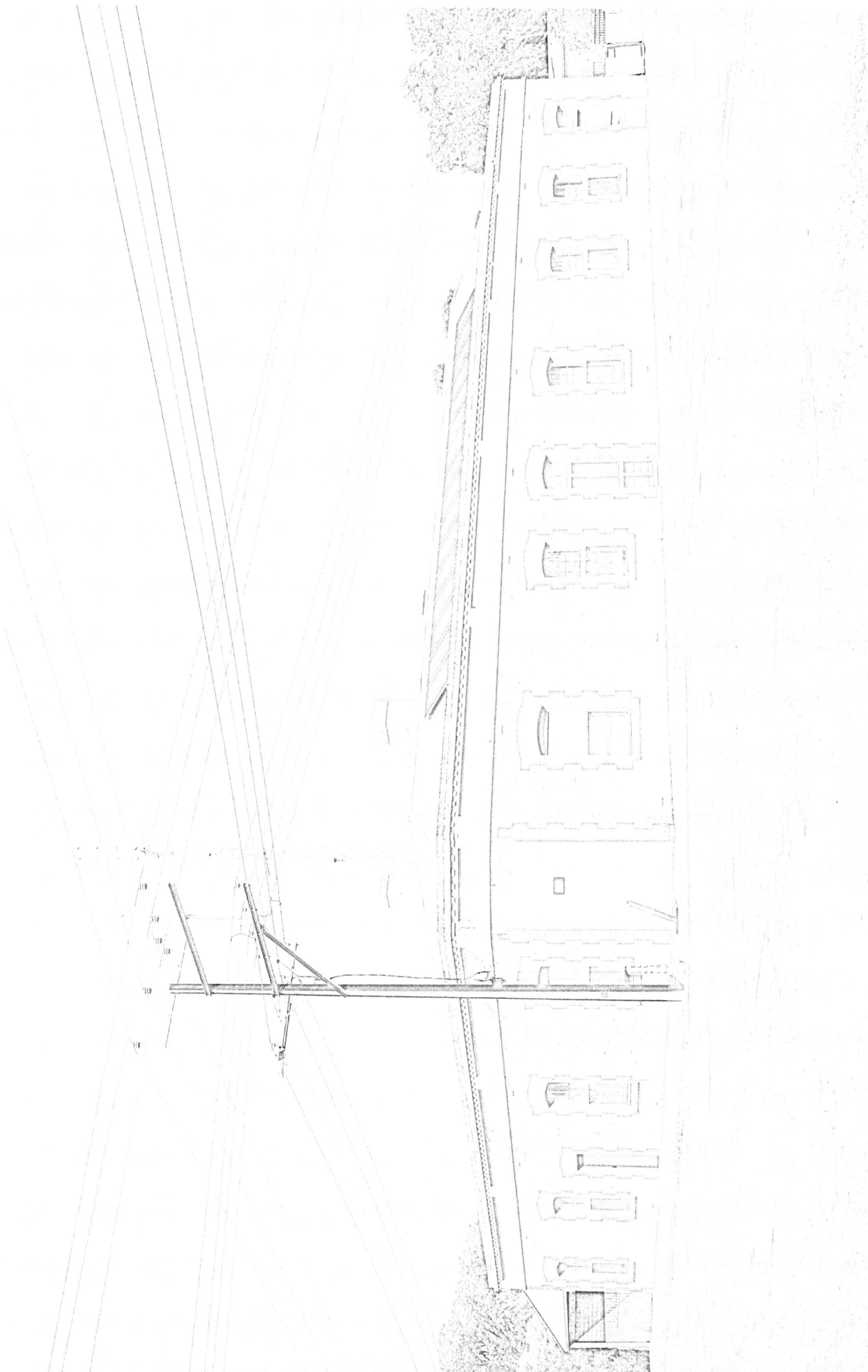

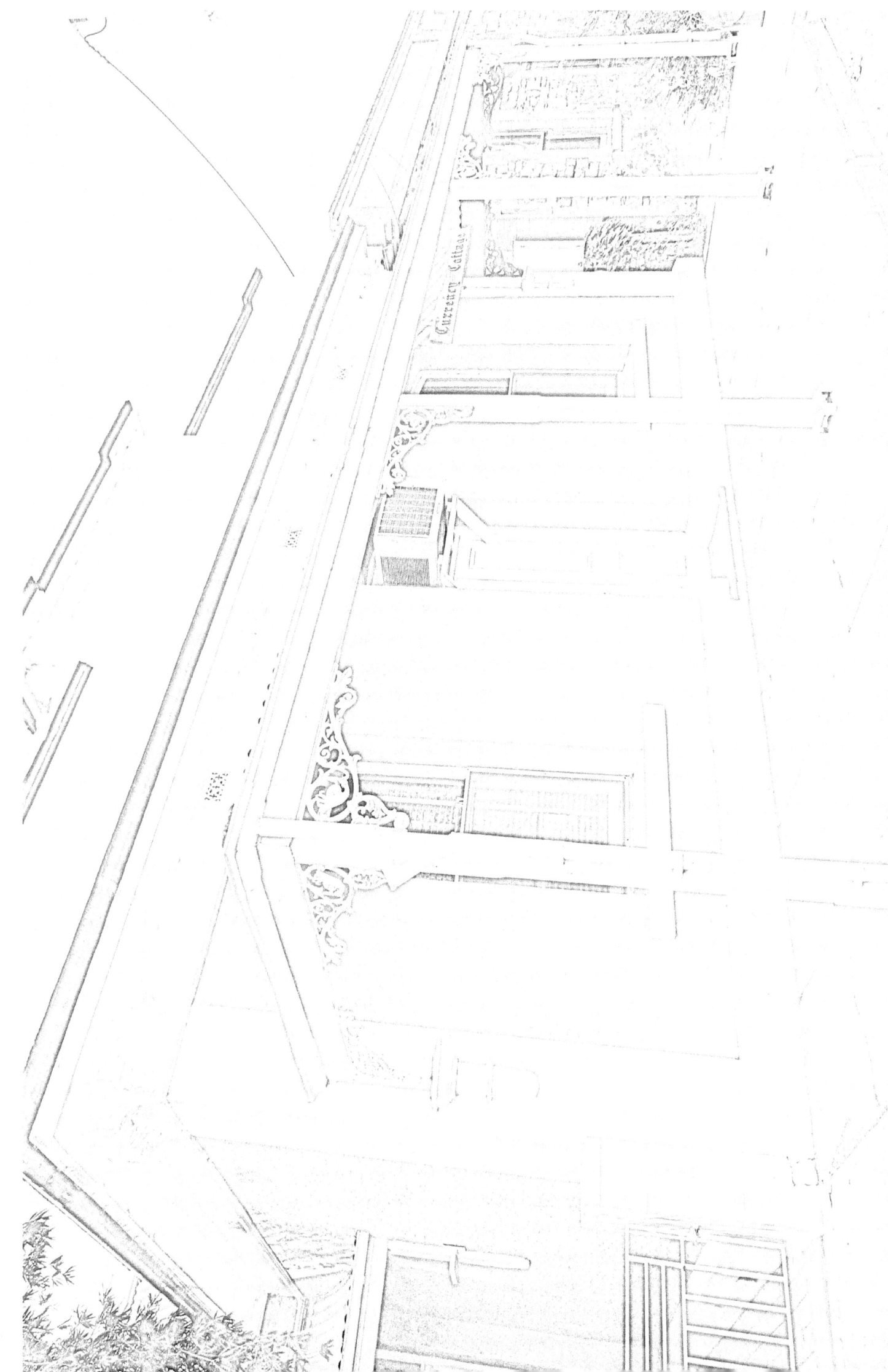

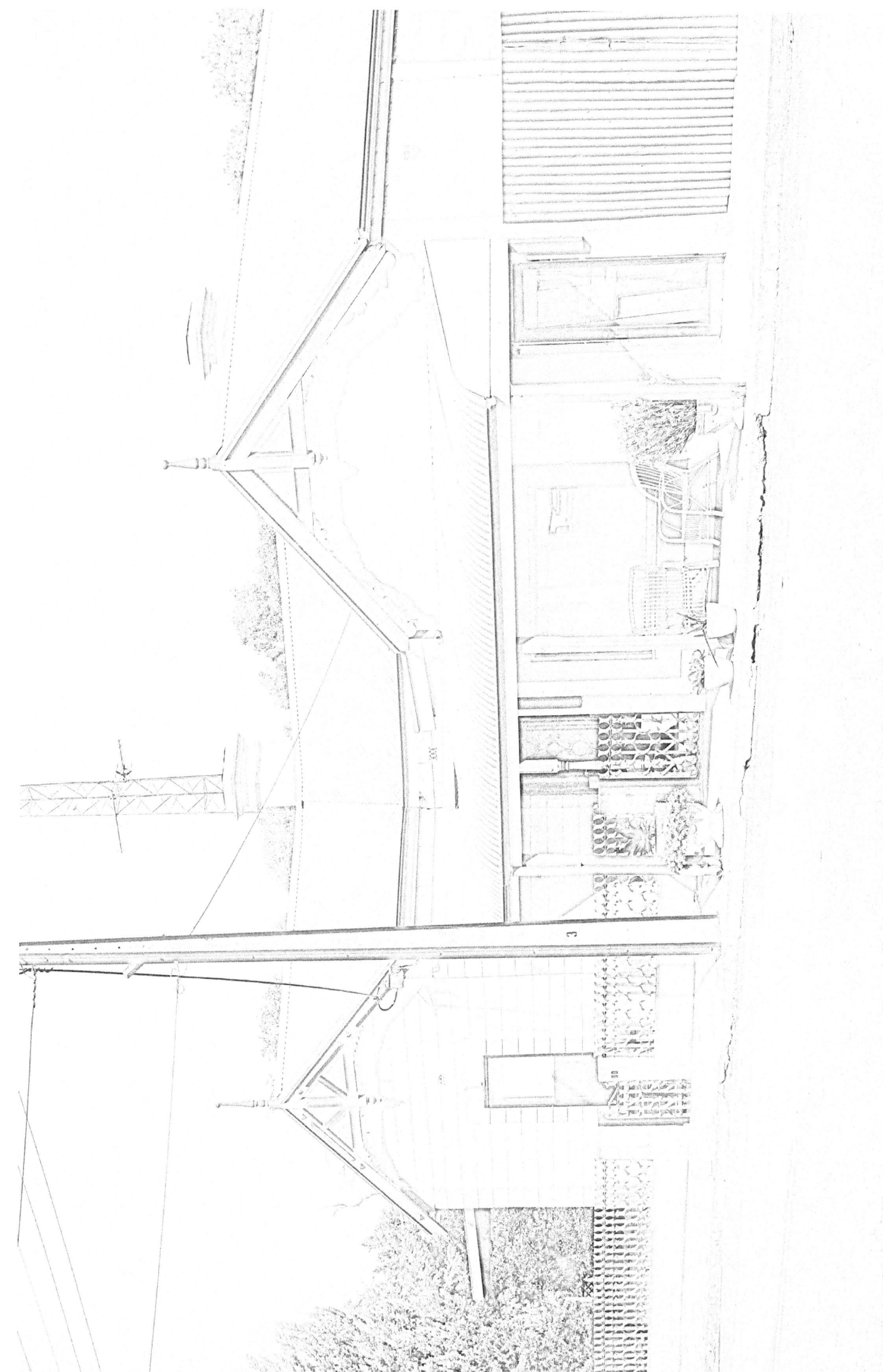

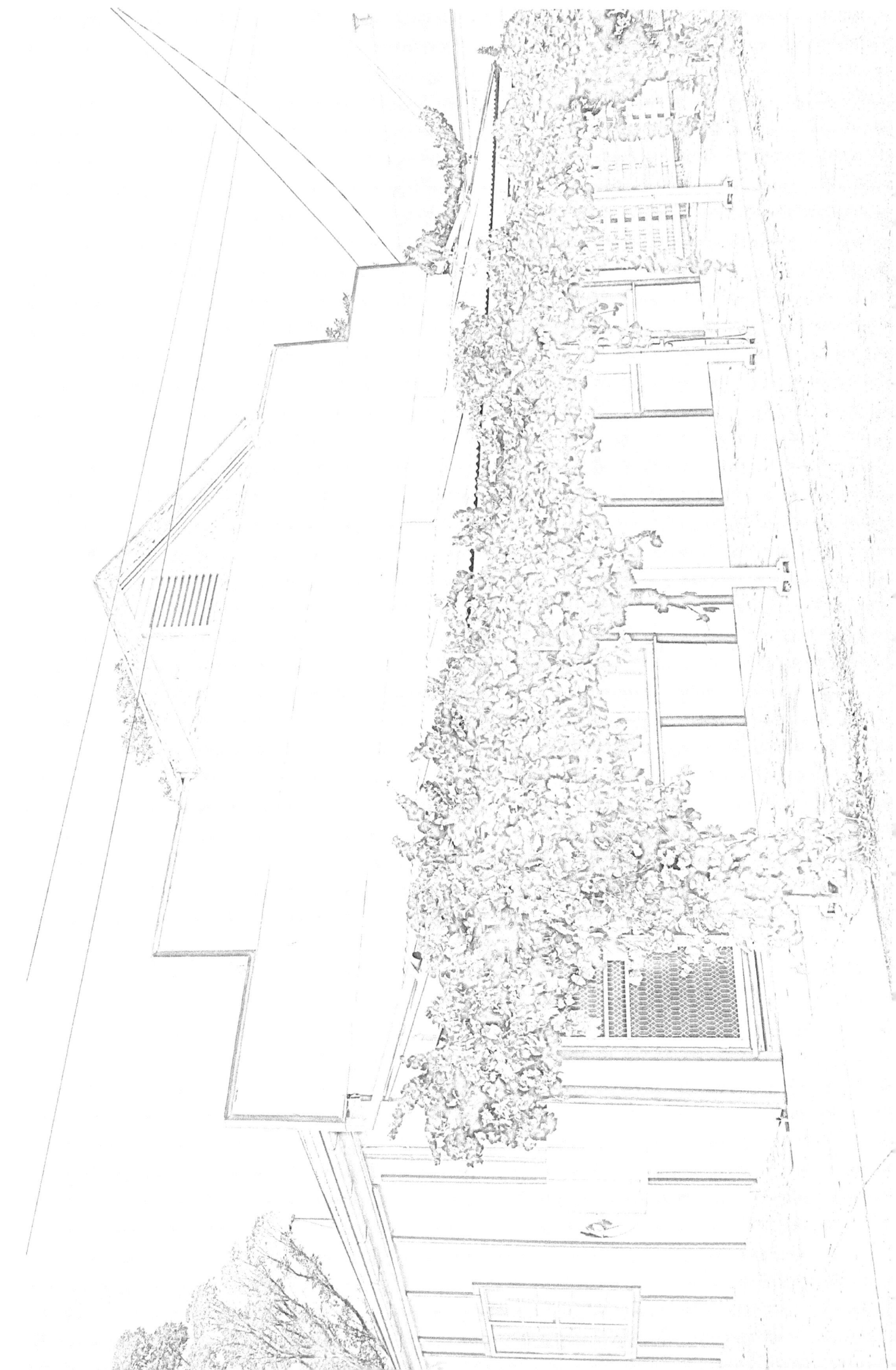

DON'T DRIVE LIKE A

Country roads need safer drivers.

MAC

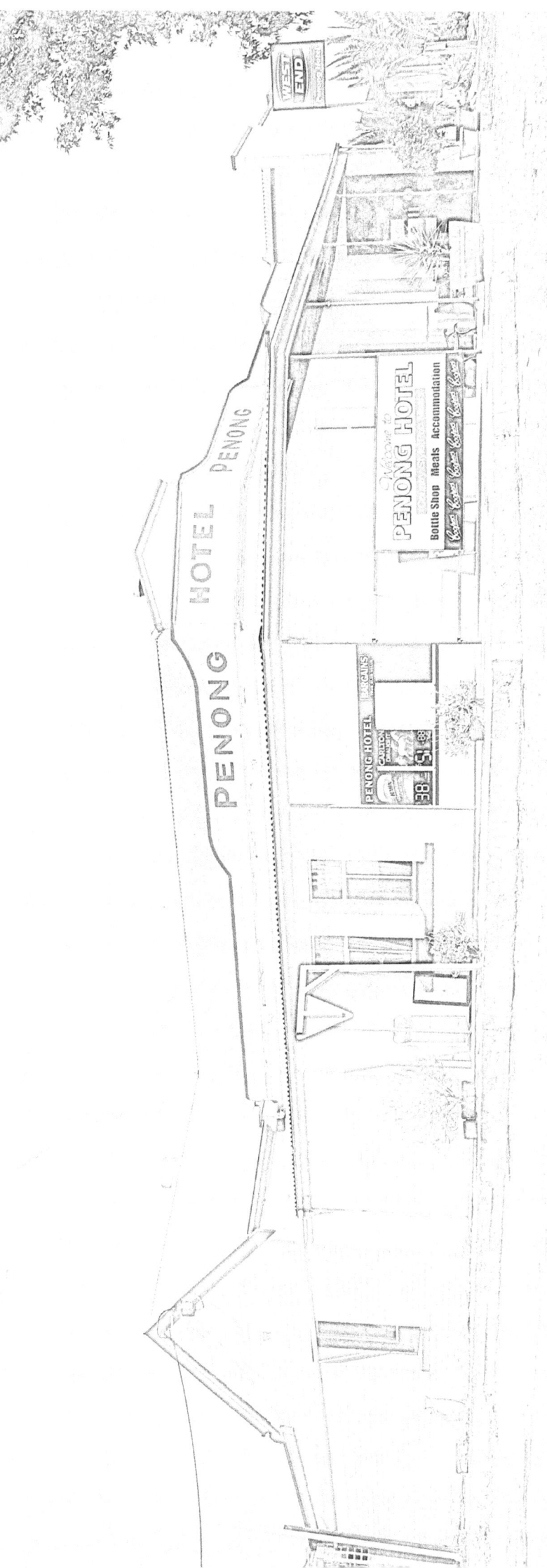

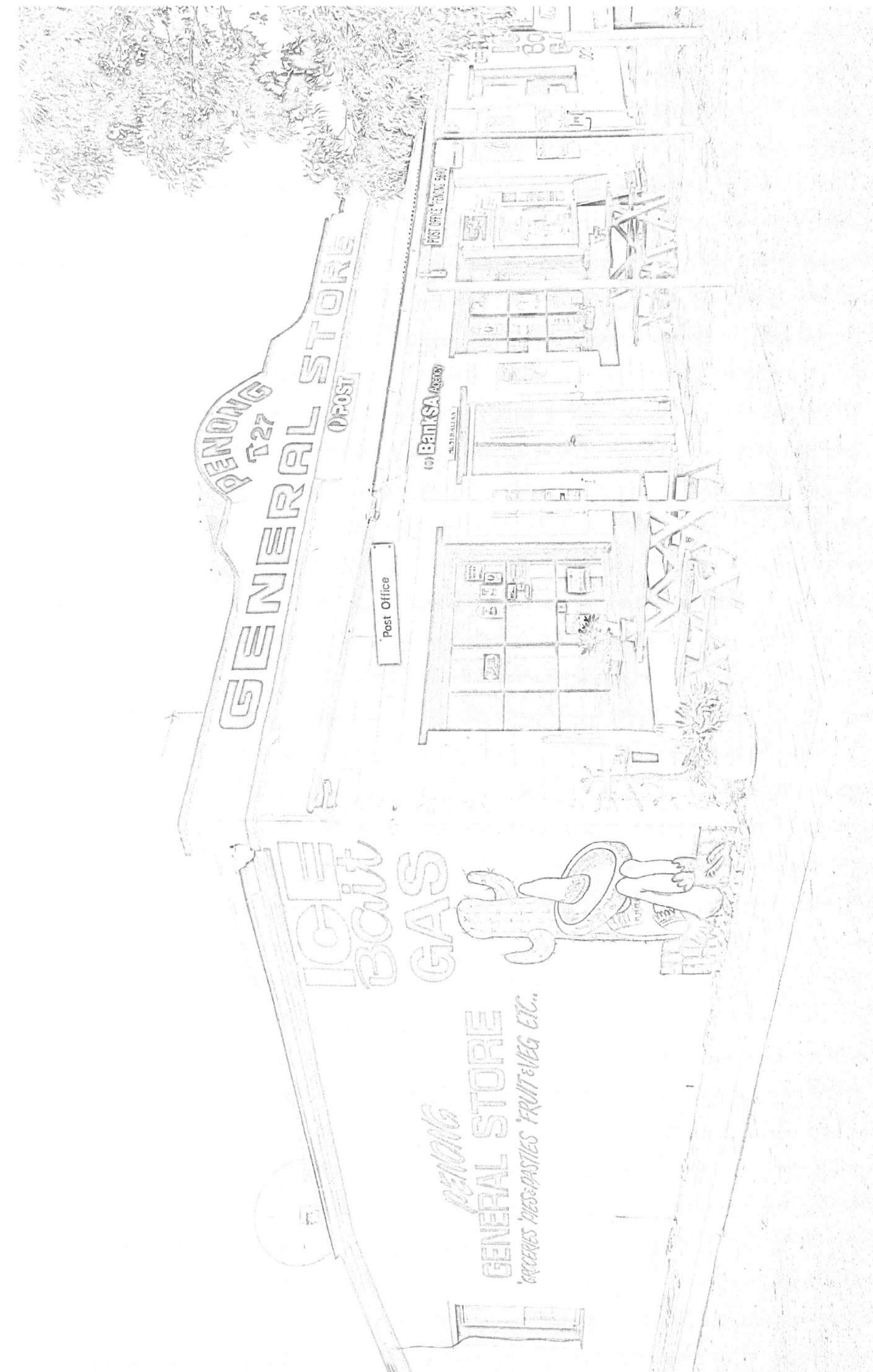

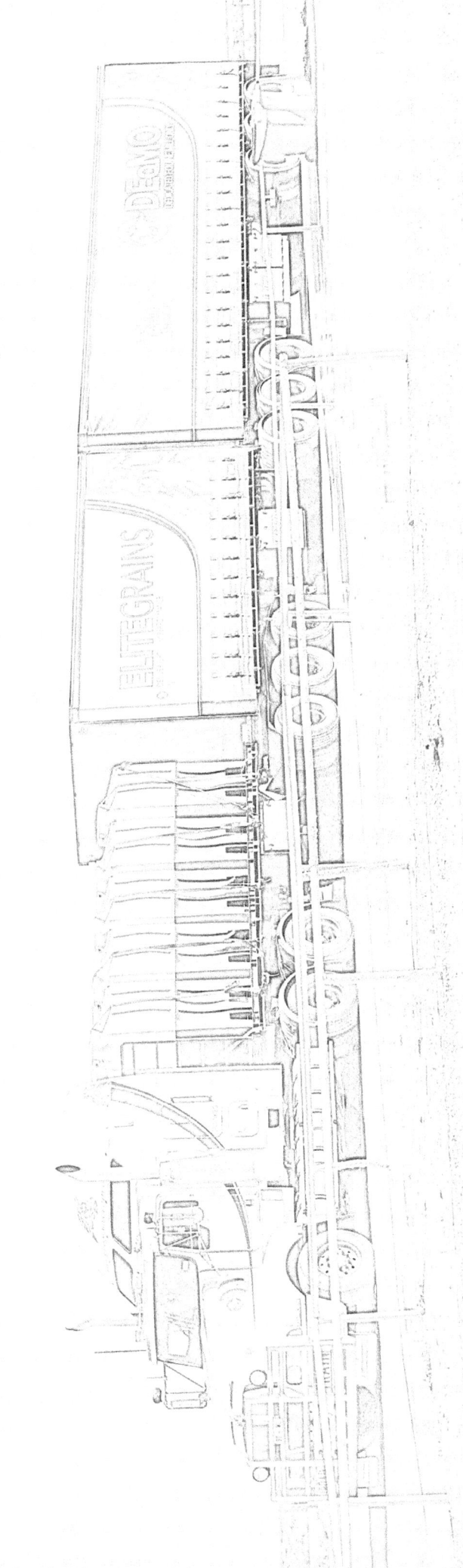

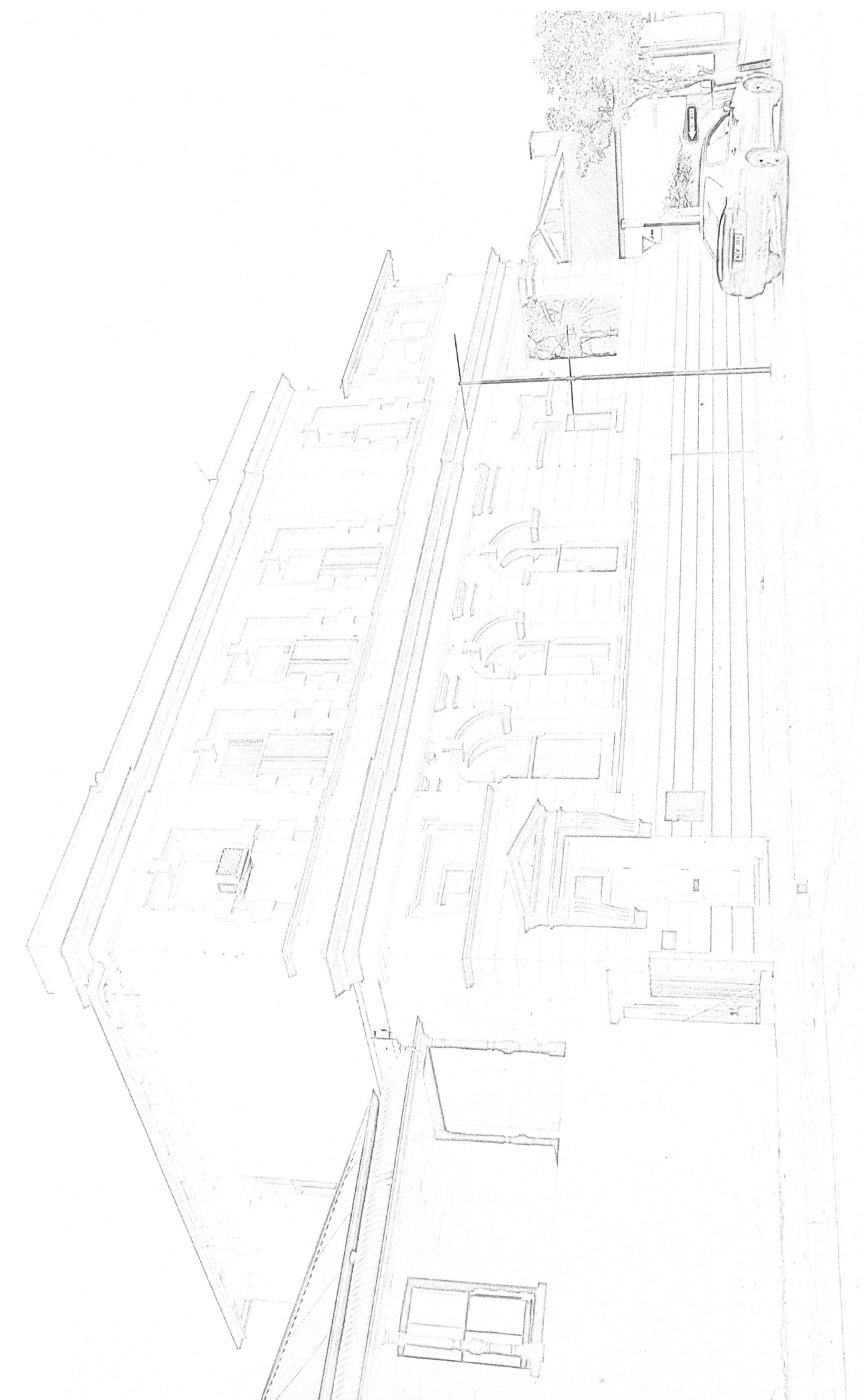

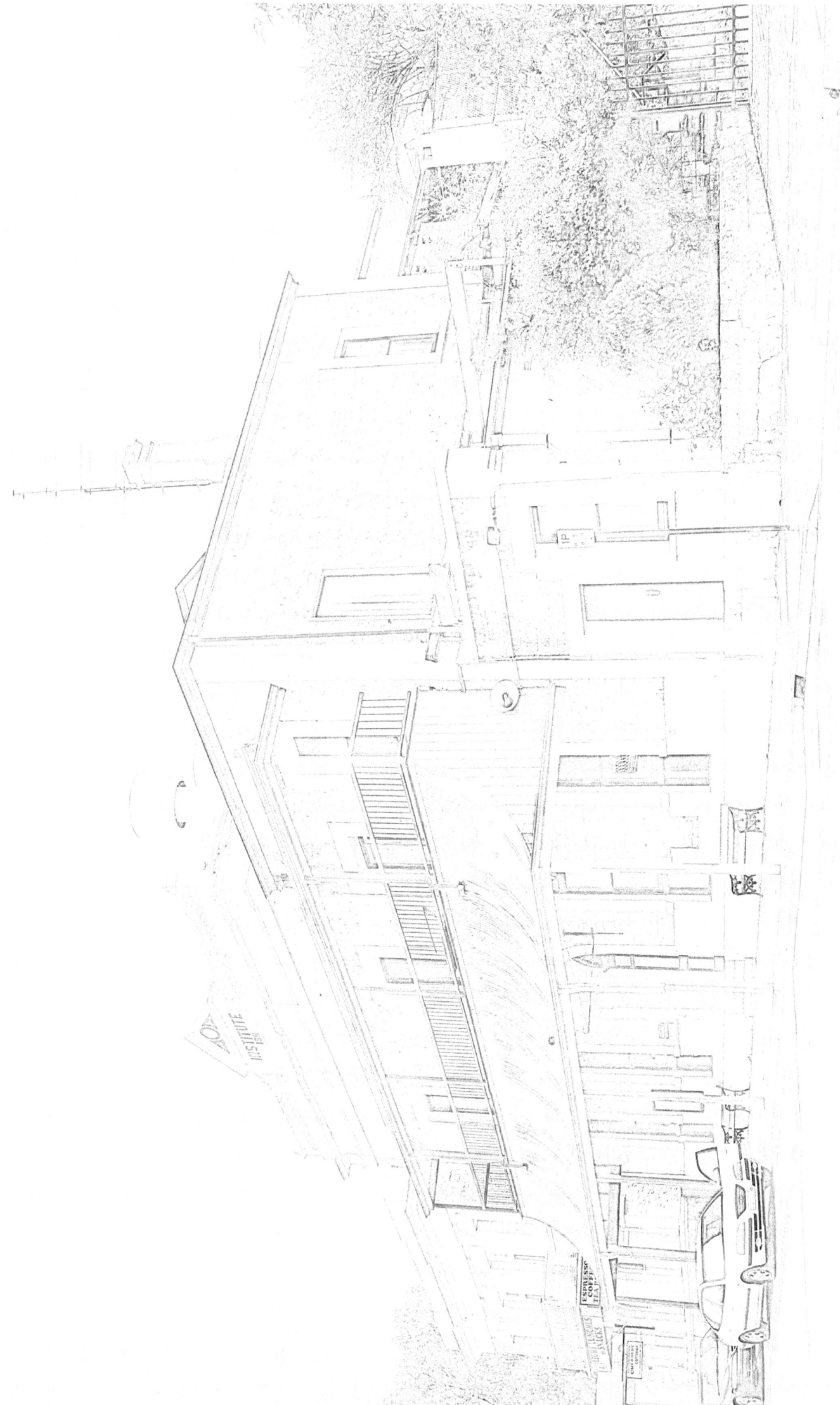

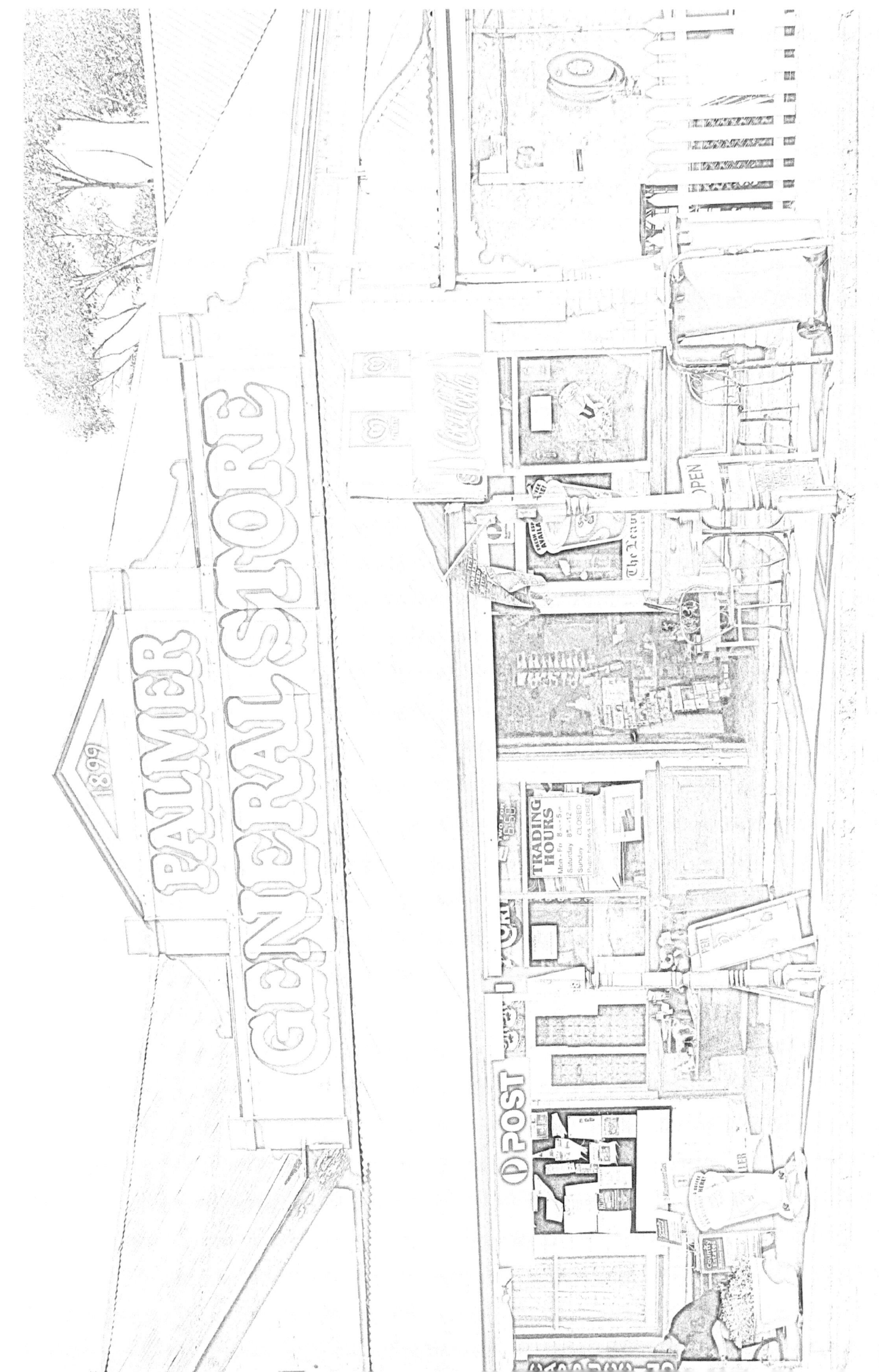

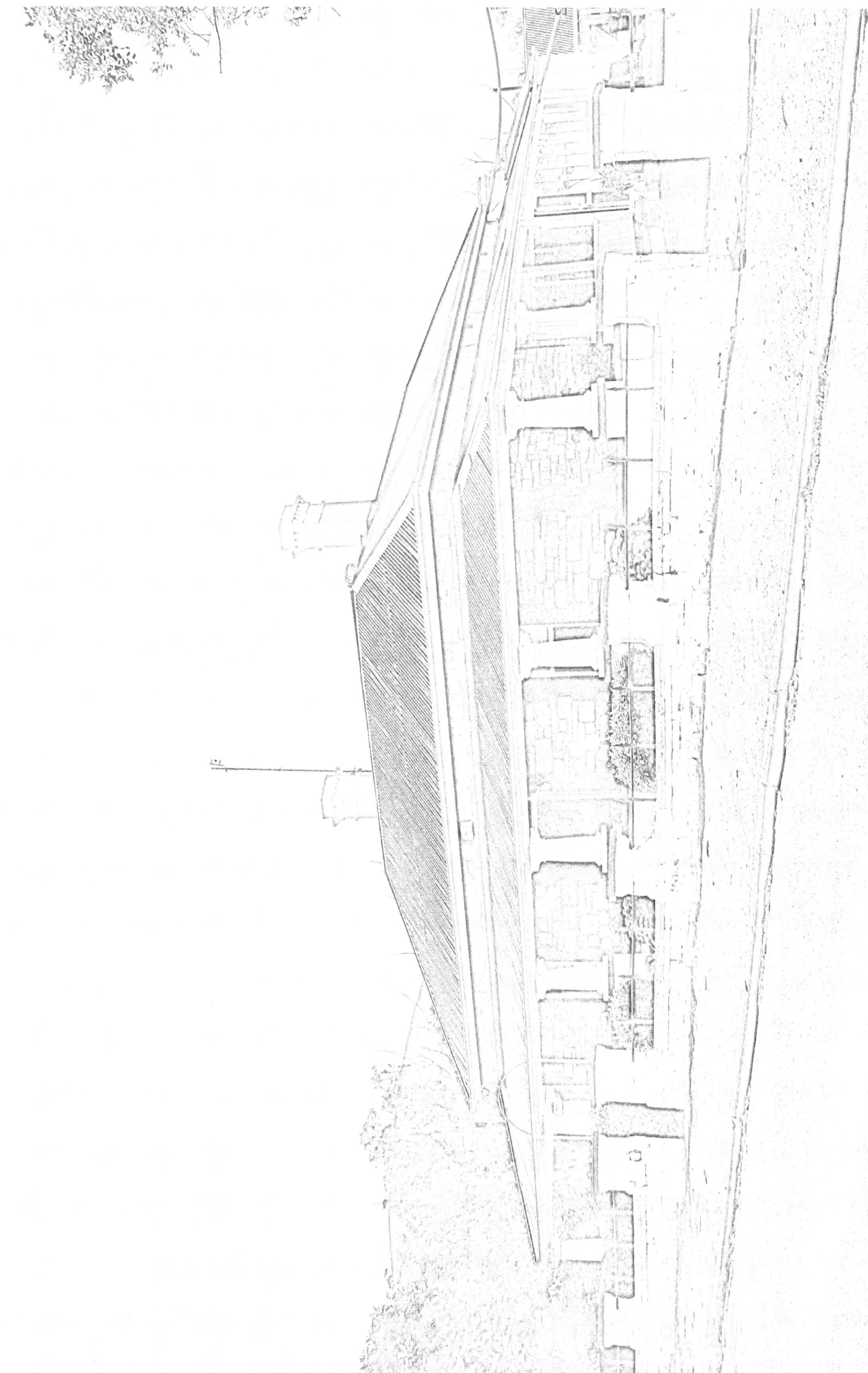

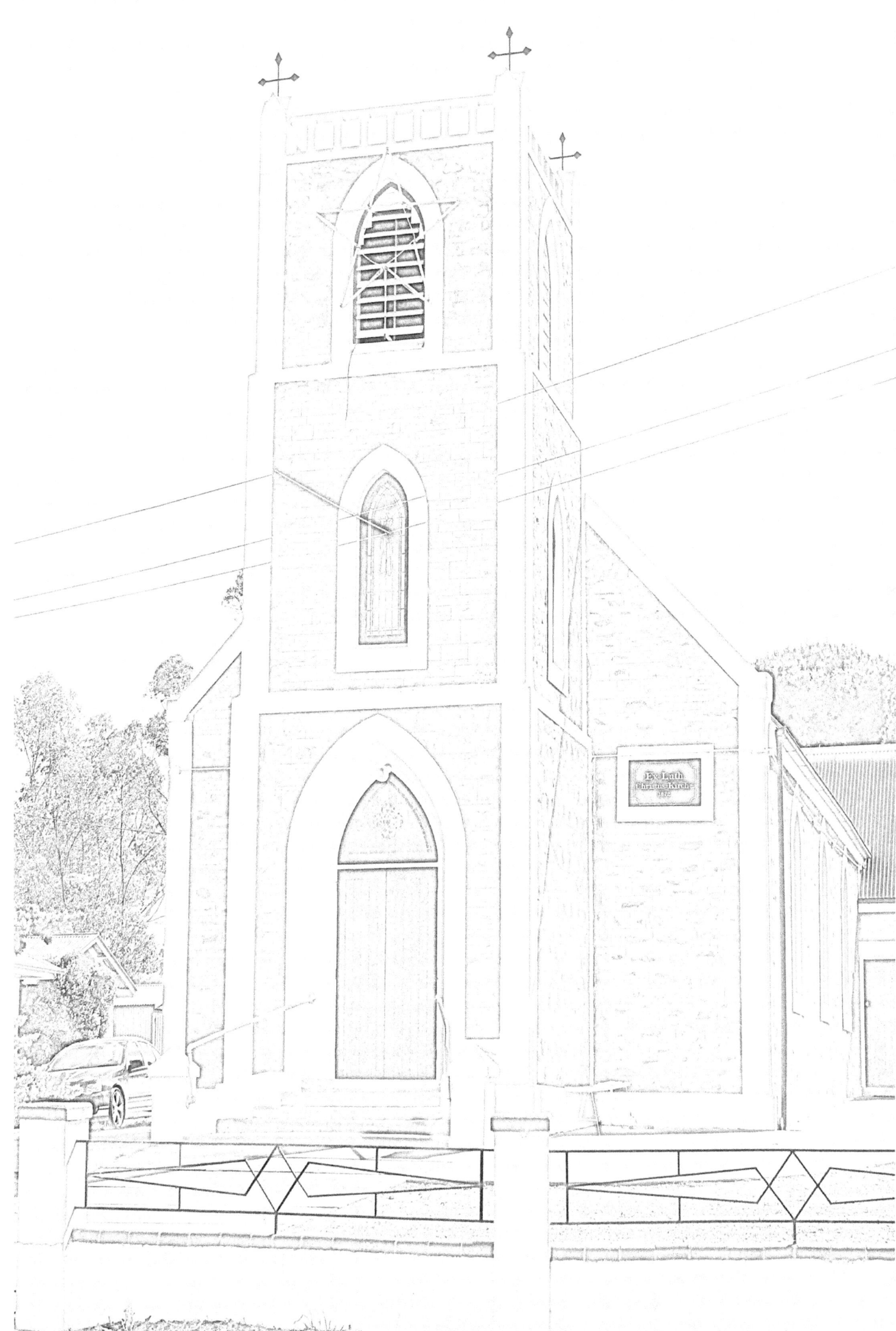

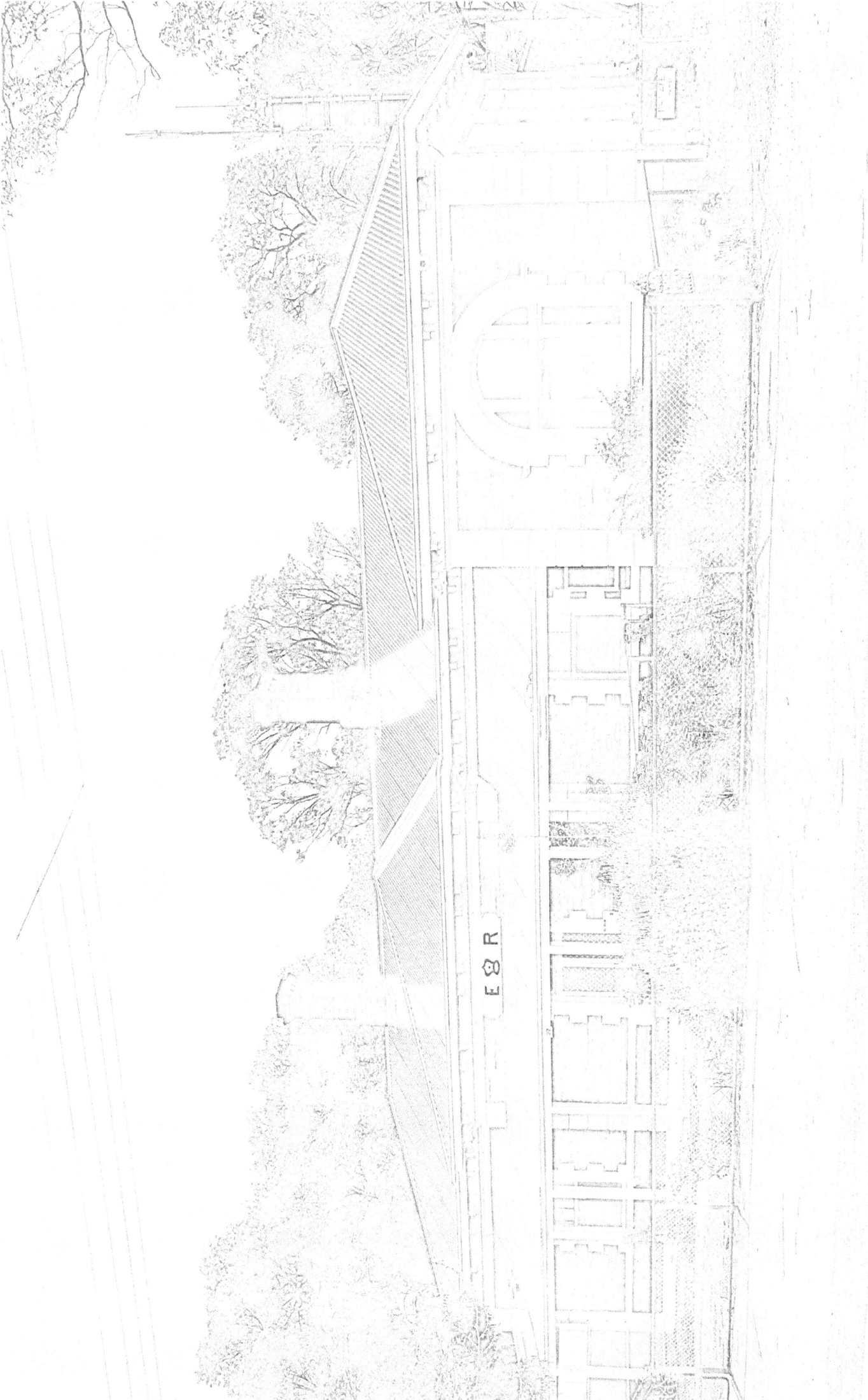

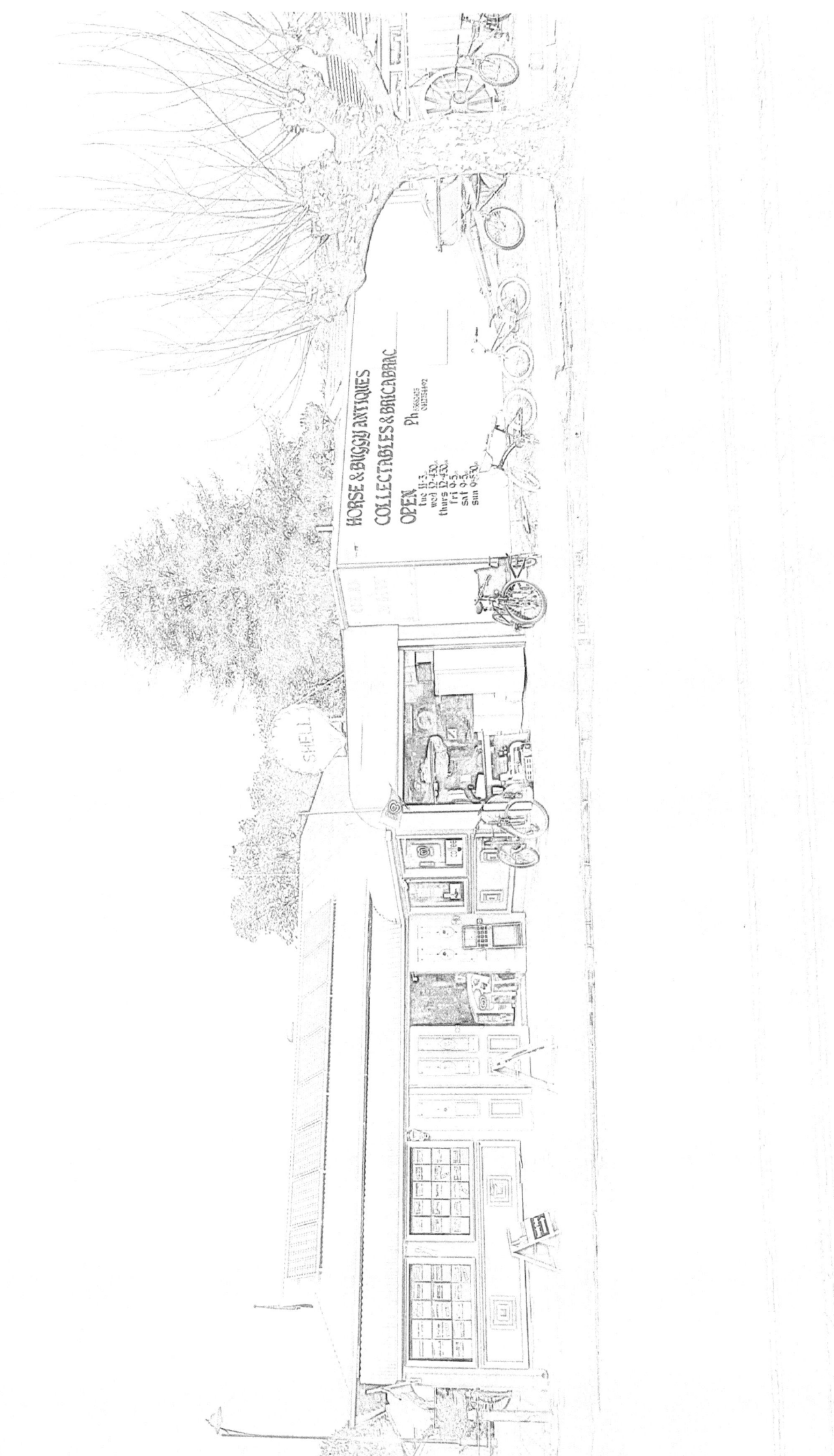

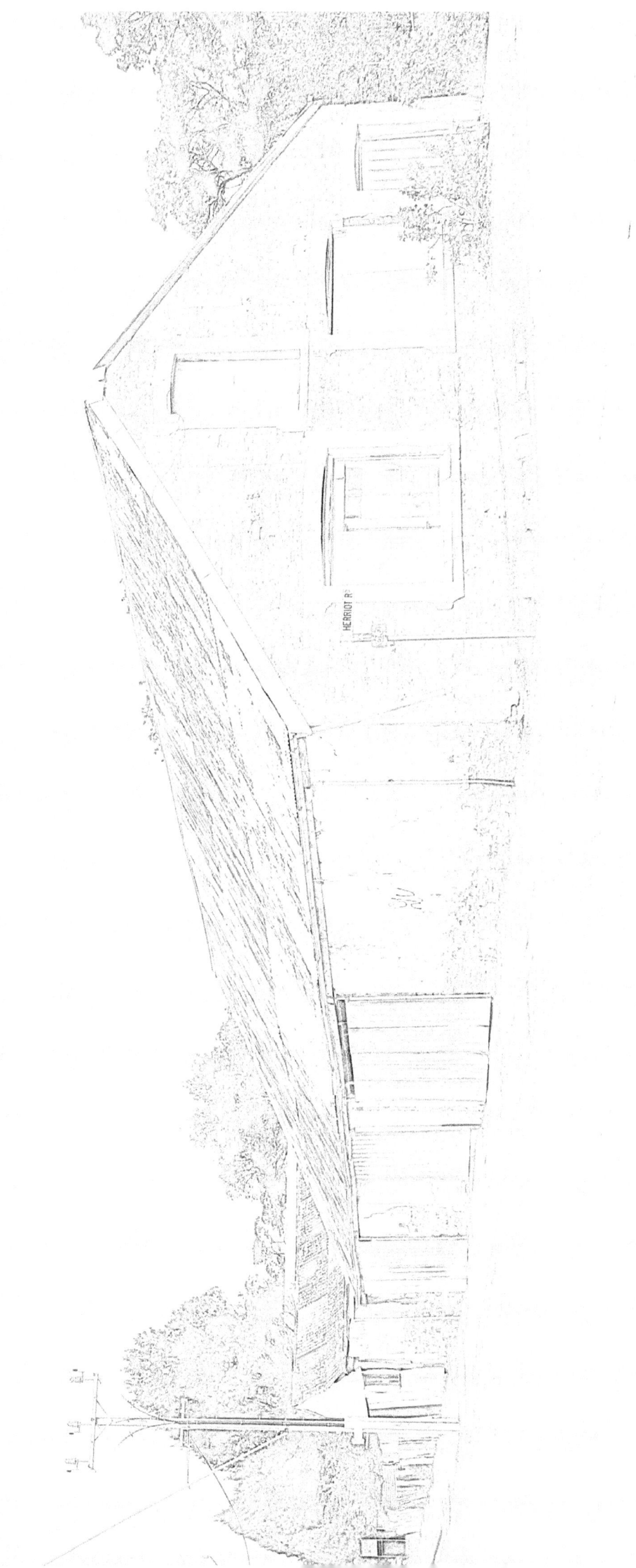

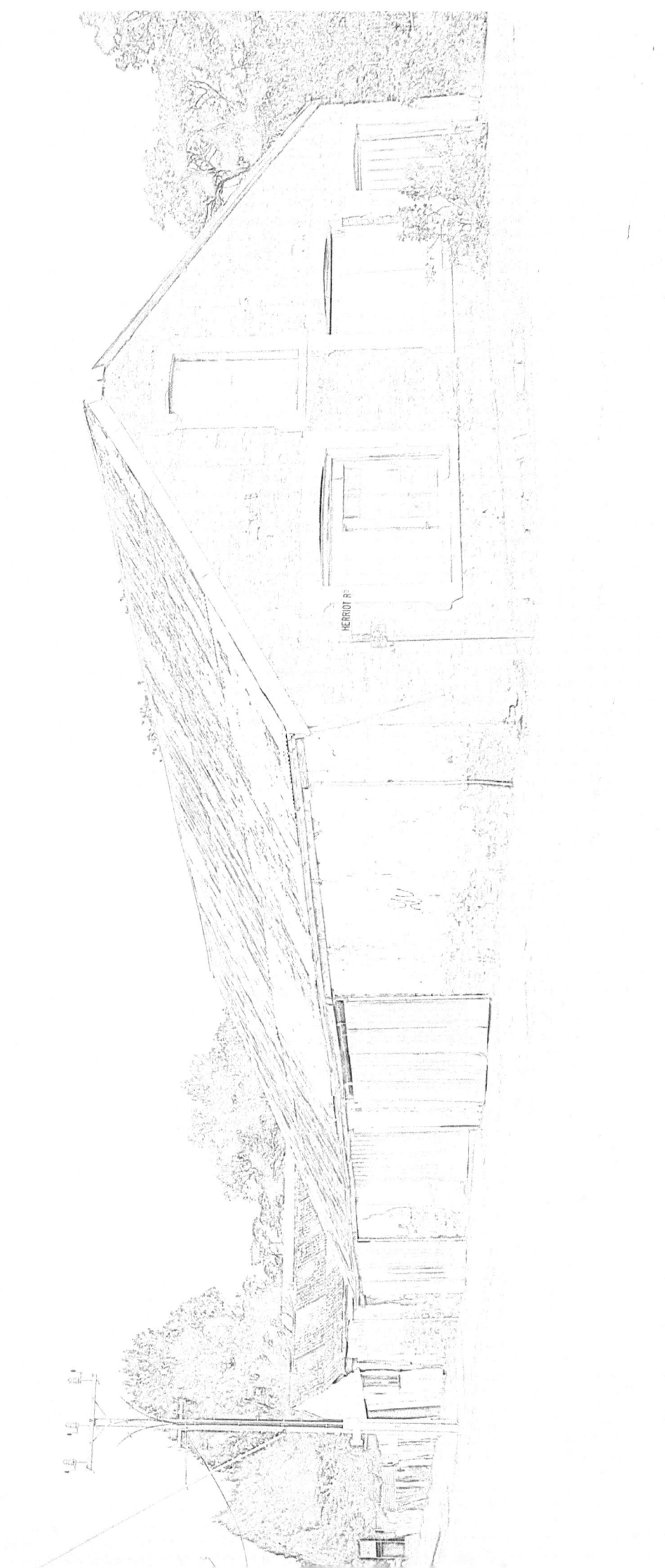

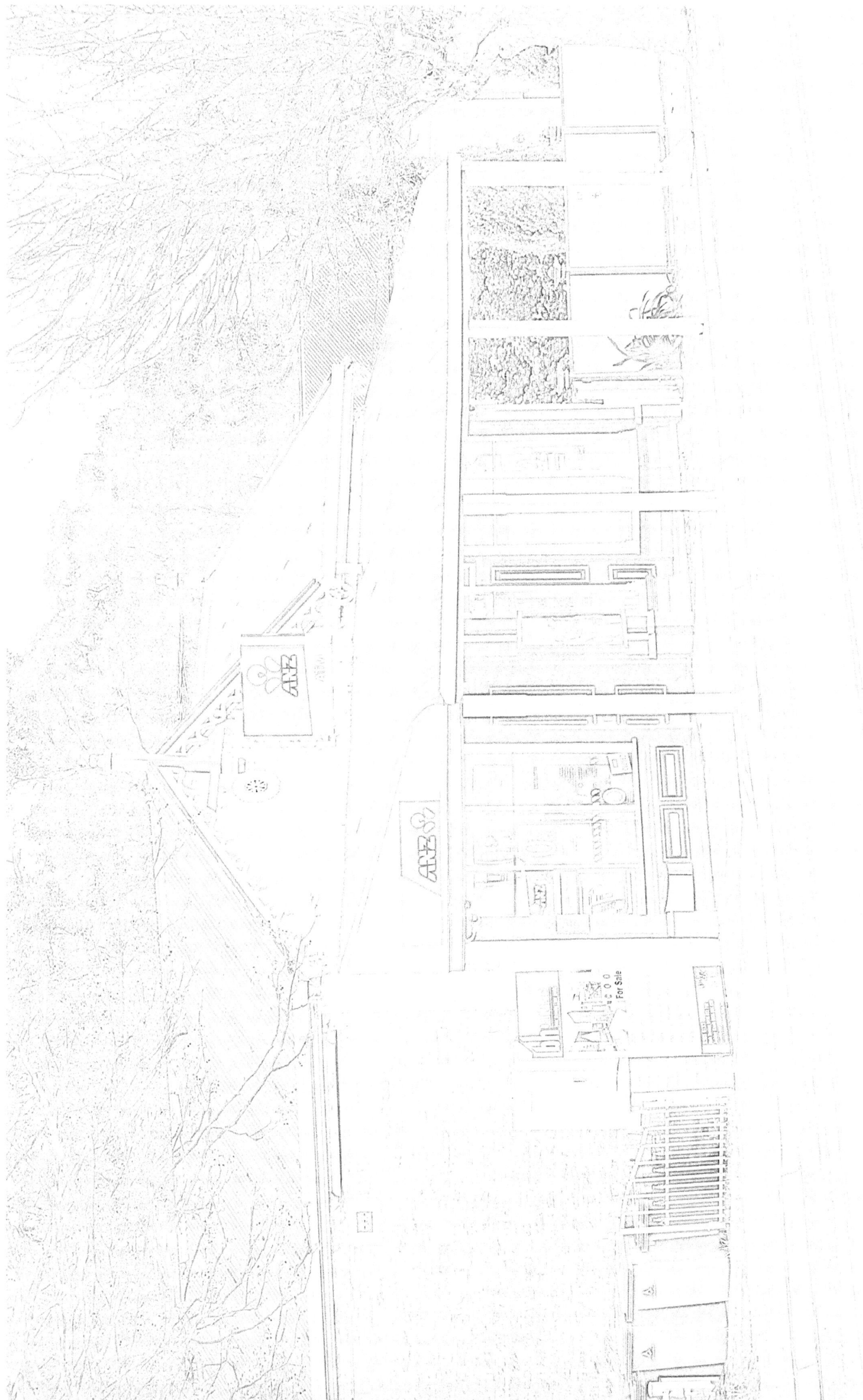